GW01606352

Modern Weightlifting and Powerlifting

MODERN WEIGHTLIFTING AND POWERLIFTING

George Popplewell

Director of Physical Recreation, University of Kent

FABER AND FABER
London Boston

First published in 1978
by Faber and Faber Limited
3 Queen Square London WC1
Printed in Great Britain by
Latimer Trend & Company Ltd Plymouth

British Library Cataloguing in Publication Data

Popplewell, George
Modern weightlifting and powerlifting.
1. Weight lifting
I. Title
796.4'1 GV546

ISBN 0-571-10760-5

Foreword

It is with pleasure that I can accept this invitation to pen the Foreword to *Modern Weightlifting and Powerlifting* for it gives me an opportunity to comment on the author as well as the work. At present the sport of weightlifting is very popular and many books are appearing on the subject, so one must ask 'Why should this book be any better than the rest?' Well, George Popplewell has a background as a physical educationist that is more acceptable than most, at least to the readers for whom this book is intended. He is a former British record holder, universities' champion, International Referee in powerlifting and weightlifting, Staff Coach of the British Amateur Weight Lifters' Association (B.A.W.L.A.) and weightlifting adviser to British universities and colleges. In addition he was the Home Office representative on the B.A.W.L.A. Central Council for many years. In 1975 he was chosen by the B.A.W.L.A. at the request of the British Council to undertake a tour of India, where he conducted clinics for coaches and training camps for national teams.

For over twenty years I have had the pleasure of his friendship and advice, and his company on many trips concerned with weightlifting. I feel this book in many ways reflects him as thoughtful, methodical, scientific and up to date.

I feel a short résumé of his experience as known to me would be of help as it shows his development as a sportsman, teacher and administrator. He gained his formal physical education qualifications at Loughborough College and Leeds University. Later he received his master's degree in education at Leicester University. He is a Fellow of the Physical Education Association. On his way to the University of Kent he was commissioned in the Royal Air Force, taught in secondary schools, and then worked for several years in the physical education branch of what was then the Prison Commission. As a sportsman he was an accomplished all-rounder, being proficient in athletics, judo, rugger and swimming. At the same time he managed to break numerous British lightheavyweight records in weightlifting. I remember coaching him in Moscow in 1957 when I discovered he was the calmest athlete when under pressure that I have ever met. He is considered among the élite of B.A.W.L.A. coaches, and I have no hesitation in recommending this book for coaches and lifters as well as for all interested in the subject.

Wally Holland, O.B.E., F.A.D.O.
Secretary, *British Amateur Weightlifters Association;*
Secretary, *Commonwealth Weightlifters Association;*
Secretary, *European Powerlifting Federation;*
Vice-President, *European Weightlifting Federation;*
Vice-President, *International Powerlifting Federation;*
Executive Member, *International Weightlifting Federation;*
President of Technical Committee of the European Weightlifting Federation.

Contents

Foreword page 7

Illustrations 13

1. **Competitive Lifting** 15

International Weightlifting Federation; International Powerlifting Federation; Rising International Standards; Lifting in Britain; Incentive Schemes; Schoolboys' Weight-training and Lifting Awards; Certificates of Merit: *B.A.W.L.A. Grading and Incentive Scheme*

2. **General Principles I** 21

Weight-training, a prerequisite to Lifting; Personal Requirements: *Dedication; Will power; Concentration; Courage; Learning Ability*; Physical Fitness: *Muscular Power; Muscular Strength; Muscular Endurance; Cardiovascular Endurance; Neuromuscular Co-ordination; Flexibility;* Tests

3. **General Principles II** 27

Further Strength Considerations: *Olympic lifts; Power Lifts;* Basic Mechanical Principles: *Force; Weight; Centre of Gravity; Gravity Line; Lever; Moment of Force; Power; Impulse; Classes of Levers; Power and Weight Arms; Balance; Reactive Force; Direction of Application of Force; Inertia; Linear and Angular Motion; Percussion Centre;* Weightlifting Skill: *Neurological Points; Skill and Learning; Skills Coaching Advice*

4. **Making a Start** 37

Adolescents; Safety Precautions: *Personal Safety Precautions; External Safety Precautions;* Equipment; Personal Kit; Basic Terminology; Where to Train; A First Weight-training Schedule; An Intermediate Weight-training Schedule; Starting to Train for Incentives or Competition

5. Weightlifting: Two Hands' Snatch 47
The Olympic Lifts: *General Rules;* Two Styles of Snatch; International Rules for the Two Hands' Snatch; Incorrect Movements; Technique: *Starting Position; Pull; Arm and Wrist Action; Receiving Positions; Recovery; Breathing; Lowering of the Weight; Procedure for Incomplete Lifts;* Comments on the Snatch; Assistance exercises: *Technical Assistance Exercises; Strength Assistance Exercises; Power Assistance Exercises; Flexibility Exercises;* Training Methods: *A Beginner's Schedule; Progression*

6. Weightlifting: Two Hands' Clean and Jerk 62
International Rules for the Two Hands' Clean and Jerk; Incorrect Movements: *Clean; Jerk;* Technique of the Clean: *Starting Position; Pull; Arm and Wrist Action; Receiving Positions; Recovery;* Technique of the Jerk: *Breathing; Procedure for Incomplete Lifts;* Comments on the Clean and Jerk; Assistance Exercises: *Technical Assistance Exercises; Strength Assistance Exercises; Power Assistance Exercises;* Training Methods: *A Beginner's Schedule*

7. Weightlifting: Advanced Training Methods 74
Training Cycles; Training Cycle Phases: *General Preparation; Strength Build-up; Strength and Technique; Competition Preparation;* Reducing Bodyweight; Warming-up; Starting Poundages

8. Lifting: Other Factors Affecting Performance 86
Staleness; Smoking; Alcohol; Diet; Personal Hygiene; Doping; Injuries; Psychological Factors

9. Powerlifting: Deep Knees' Bend (Squat) 94
International Rules; Causes for Disqualification; Technique of the Squat: *Preparation; Starting Position; Recovery;* Remarks; Assistance Exercises; Training methods: *A Beginner's Schedule*

10. Powerlifting: Bench Press 99
International Rules; Causes for Disqualification; Technique of the Bench Press: *Preparation; The Pressing Movement;* Remarks; Assistance Exercises; Training Methods: *A Beginner's Schedule*

11. Powerlifting: Dead Lift 106

International Rules; Causes for Disqualification; Technique of the Dead Lift: *Preparation; The Lifting Movement; Lowering the Weight;* Remarks; Assistance Exercises; Training Methods: *A Beginner's Schedule*

12. Powerlifting: Advanced Training Methods 110

Advanced Schedules for the Squat; Advanced Schedules for the Bench Press; Advanced Schedules for the Dead Lift; Composite Schedules for Powerlifters; Competition Preparation

13. Teaching Weightlifting 116

Reasons for Teaching Weightlifting; Teaching Weightlifting in Schools and Colleges: *Equipment; Organization; Standing in;* Lesson Plans: *A Weight-training Lesson for Beginners; Lessons for Intermediate Pupils; First-stage Weightlifting Lessons for Beginners; Second-stage Weightlifting Lessons for Beginners;* Teaching Methods: *Class-teaching Technique; Whole-part-whole Method; Phase Method; Trial and Error Method;* Advanced coaching; Weightlifting Competitions in Schools, Colleges and Clubs: *Competition Procedure; Handicap; Attempts;* Coaching Aids

14. Weightlifting for the Disabled 128

General Background; Objectives; Competitive Weightlifting: *Categories;* Rules for the Lifts and Methods of Performance: *Paraplegic Press on Bench; Pull Over and Press on Back; Lateral Raise, Lying;* Training Methods for Disabled Lifters: *Beginners; Progression; Advanced Training*

Appendix Dimensions of Apparatus for Paraplegic Weightlifting 136

Further Reading 137

Index 139

Illustrations

PLATES (*between pages 62 and 63*)

1. Assorted weight-training equipment
2. Weightlifting equipment
3. The Bulgarian electrodinamograph
4. Squat stands and Kolev (Bulgaria) push jerking
5. Reverse curl—starting position
6. Reverse curl—finishing position
7. Upright rowing—starting position
8. Upright rowing—finishing position
9. Press behind neck—starting position
10. Press behind neck—finishing position
11. The 'get set' position of Stan Stanzyck (U.S.A.)
12. Kailajarvi (Finland) demonstrating the snatch pull
13. Pervushin (U.S.S.R.) during the snatch pull
14. Rigert (U.S.S.R.) in the squat snatch receiving position
15. George Newton (Great Britain) snatching
16. Palinski (Poland) cleaning a World Record
17. Baszanowski (Poland) pulling in the Clean
18. Heuser (G.D.R.) in the clean pull
19. Rigert (U.S.S.R.) in the squat Clean
20. Shopov (Bulgaria) jerking at the 1972 Olympic Games
21. Split snatch balance exercise—start
22. Split snatch balance exercise—finish
23. Squat snatch balance exercise—behind neck start
24. Squat snatch balance exercise—in front of neck start
25. Squat snatch balance exercise—finish
26. Split lunges—start
27. Split lunges—finish
28. Push Jerk—preliminary dip
29. Push Jerk—finish
30. Half Squat
31. 'Good morning' exercise—start
32. Prone hyperextension—finish
33. Thigh-suppling exercise
34. Shoulder-mobilizing exercise
35. Squat—taking the bar from the stands

36. Start of the Squat
37. Squat with tops of thighs below horizontal
38. Loaders handing barbell to lifter for Bench Press
39. Bench Press—just before upward drive
40. Bench Press—during upward drive
41. Finish of the Bench Press
42. Start of the Dead Lift
43. Finish of the Dead Lift
44. A heavy Dead Lift
45. Starting position of paraplegic Bench Press
46. Paraplegic Bench Press
47. Starting position of the Lateral Raise, Lying
48. Finish of the Lateral Raise, Lying
49. The pull over of the Pull Over and Press on Back
50. The press of the Pull Over and Press on Back
51. Finish of the press
52. Start of the dumb-bells Press on Back
53. Finish of the dumb-bells Press on Back

FIGURES

1. Classes of lever — *page* 31
2. Mechanically balanced 'get set' position — 32
3. Reactive force through a lifter's feet — 33
4. Feet in the split snatch receiving position — 52
5. Feet in the squat snatch receiving position — 53
6*a*. Sequence of movement of the split Snatch
b. Sequence of movement of the squat Snatch — 54
7*a*. Sequence of movement of the split Clean
b. Sequence of movement of the squat Clean — 67
c. Sequence of movement of the Jerk
8. Sequence of movement of the Squat — 96
9*a*. Sequence of movement of the Bench Press
b. End view of the Bench Press — 102
10. Alternative version of the Bench Press
11. Sequence of movement of the Dead Lift — 107
12. The Murray Cross — 126

One Competitive Lifting

International Weightlifting Federation

In 1920, the International Weightlifting Federation (Fédération Halterophile Internationale), or I.W.F. for short, was formed. Over one hundred national amateur federations such as the American Athletic Union (A.A.U.) and the British Amateur Weight Lifters' Association (B.A.W.L.A.) comprise the I.W.F., which organizes, controls and develops weightlifting on an international scale, including World Championships and the Olympic Games. The I.W.F. sets up the technical rules for weightlifting and keeps a register of World records. It is recognized by the International Olympic Committee (I.O.C.) and follows the Olympic ethic in all its activities. The steering and management committee of the I.W.F. consists of a president, six vice-presidents, seven members, a general secretary/treasurer and an assistant secretary.

The ultimate power of the I.W.F. is its Congress which takes place every four years at the time of the World Championships or Olympic Games. At the Congress officers are elected and I.W.F. articles and rules may be modified. Also, member nations can put forward proposals to the Congress for inclusion on the agenda: discussion and voting then take place in a constitutional fashion. During periods between Congresses, the I.W.F. is administered by a Bureau.

The Congress appoints Technical and Medical Committees. The Technical Committee is concerned with the provision, instruction and examination of referees, the publishing of technical material on the organization of competition, and the dispensing of information on modern systems of training and performance of lifts. The Medical Committee is concerned with the health of lifters and is involved in the doping control procedure. Also, the Medical Committee collects data on the long-term effects of weightlifting on the human organism, besides studying sports' medicine and specific injuries.

International Powerlifting Federation

A comparatively new organization, the International Powerlifting Federation (I.P.F.) was formed in 1972. Its main aim is to provide powerlifters with an opportunity to compete internationally. In recent years, powerlifting has attracted many followers, especially from the bodybuilding ranks. Sometimes lifters successfully combine Olympic weightlifting with powerlifting—for example, Precious McKenzie, M.B.E., the British and Commonwealth Olympic weightlifting champion and World powerlifting champion in the 52 kg (114½ lb) class.

It is hoped that the World Powerlifting Championships will be held in a different country each year. It should be mentioned that there are many Divisional Championships from which finalists are selected for National Championships. Those reaching the appropriate qualifying totals in the latter are selected for the World Powerlifting Championships.

But will this branch of the sport ever attain Olympic Games status? The numbers that participate suggest that powerlifting deserves support and backing at national level. Powerlifting has a strong following in Australia, Canada, Finland, France, Great Britain, Holland, Italy, Jamaica, Mexico, New Zealand, Norway, Puerto Rico, South Africa, Sweden, U.S.A, Zambia and other countries.

The power lifts are the Deep Knees' Bend (Squat), the Press on Bench and the Dead Lift. The rules, techniques and training methods are described in Chapters 9–12.

Rising International Standards

Modern training methods, techniques, competitions of various levels, improved equipment and greater knowledge of the preparation of lifters have all contributed to the phenomenal increases in weightlifting performance in the last half-century. At the Antwerp Olympic Games in 1920, Bottino of Italy, weighing over 110 kg (242½ lb), lifted 120 kg (264½ lb) in the Two Hands' Clean and Jerk. At Munich in 1972 Smalcerz of Poland in the 52 kg (114¼ lb) class on the same lift hoisted 125 kg (275½ lb) overhead. Also at Munich, in the over 110 kg (242½ lb) class, Alexeev of the U.S.S.R. jerked 230 kg (506 lb).

Before the Second World War, Italy, France, Germany, Egypt and the U.S.A. were the leading nations. In the 1920s Italy and France were the dominant weightlifting nations. Italy declined towards the end of the decade, while France continued to do well in the 1930s: she gained three Olympic gold medals in 1932 and one in 1936. Germany gained gold medals in 1928, 1932 and 1936. Egypt won two gold medals in 1936 and another two in 1948. The U.S.A. did not collect any gold medals on her home ground, Los Angeles, in 1932. However, a gold was gained in 1936 when Terlazzo won the 60 kg class. In 1948, the U.S.A. was supreme in London with four Olympic gold medals to her credit. Great Britain's lifters did creditably, although she did not gain any first places in 1948; Julian Creus was placed second in the 56 kg class and Jim Halliday third in the 67·5 kg class.

In the 1950s the U.S.S.R. demonstrated her strength in the sport. There were clashes with the U.S.A. In the 1960s and early 1970s the

U.S.S.R. dominated the weightlifting world. Iron Curtain countries such as Poland, Hungary and Bulgaria won first places in both the Olympic Games and World Championships. The U.S.A., Japan, Iran, Czechoslovakia, Finland, Norway and Great Britain also won first places. At the 1974 World Championships in Manilla, Bulgaria won the team prize, forcing the U.S.S.R. into second place.

The large number of practising weightlifters (nearly half a million in the U.S.S.R.), the high standard of facilities, coaching, training methods and preparation of lifters, and the numerous competitions and contributions of scientists (including once outstanding lifters) are but a few of the reasons for the ascendancy of the U.S.S.R. and other Iron Curtain countries. Other countries are taking note by developing campaigns to raise standards. Technical and medical knowledge is important. A general public which is both informed and appreciative and takes an interest in weightlifting seems to help by giving support and acting as a stimulus. Cuba is an interesting example of what can be done in a relatively short time by applying modern weightlifting technology, finance and other resources into the weightlifting enterprise. Crash-courses for physical education teachers and the participation of youth are given priority. Not only has there been a massive increase in participation, but also standards have risen. In 1959 there were eighty-two lifters in Cuba; in 1973 this rose to thirteen thousand.

Bulgaria is another example of what can be done by thorough organization, selection and the training of youth. Selection starts with careful mass-screening tests on a large scale, followed by specialized and final selection tests. At the age of twelve, children are tested carefully for the special qualities necessary for weightlifting and then they are selected for entry to special sports schools. Finally, there is a central sports school in Sofia: its products are in the World class. However, while such a system produces incredible results it does need state backing.

Lifting in Britain

The B.A.W.L.A. is the governing body of weightlifting in Britain. It organizes National Championships in both Olympic weightlifting and powerlifting as well as selecting for international events and organizing training squads of promising lifters at schoolboy, junior (the year in which they become twenty years of age), under twenty-three and senior levels. The Divisions of the national body promote Divisional Championships besides providing referees for County and other Championships.

Not everyone specializes in the Olympic lifts or the power lifts. There is a wide variety of lifts which can be practised. Records can be attempted on some thirty-two lifts in bodyweight classes ranging from

52 kg (115 lb) to over 110 kg (242½ lb). Some of these lifts are two handed, while some are one handed. International pattern barbells are used for a number of lifts, although some specialize with dumbbells or plain barbells, depending on the lift in question. Record attempts must be performed before qualified referees, who certify the lifts. The claim for National records must be forwarded to the Registrar of British Records, or, in the case of divisional, subdivisional, county or local records, to the appropriate Divisional Registrar of Records. World or Commonwealth record claims must go to the secretary of the I.W.F. or Commonwealth W.F. for ratification.

Most lifters start their competitive careers by lifting in friendly matches for their school, college or club. Some lift in leagues, usually in teams of three, and some method of handicap is used to compare the totals lifted in relation to the combined bodyweights of the lifters. Sometimes postal competitions are held—for example, between Canadian universities where travelling is an obstacle.

More serious lifters aspire to lifting in Divisional Championships. Those reaching the appropriate qualifying totals laid down are invited to lift in the National Championships, which are held each year. These prestigious Championships are important since they form the basis of selection for teams in minor international contests and tournaments, European Championships, World Championships and the Olympic Games. The following British Olympic Weightlifting Championships are held.

Schoolboys (14–16 years of age)
Juniors (16 to the year in which they become 20 years of age)
Under 23 years of age
Seniors

The bodyweight categories for these championships are as follows: up to 52 kg (114½ lb); up to 56 kg (123¼ lb); up to 60 kg (132¼ lb); up to 67·5 kg (148¾ lb); up to 75 kg (165¼ lb); up to 82·5 kg (181¾ lb); up to 90 kg (198¼ lb); up to 100 kg (220¼ lb); up to 110 kg (242¼ lb); and 110 kg plus (242½ lb plus). To cater for lighter bodyweights than the above range, there are the following additional classes for schoolboys: up to 44 kg (96¾ lb); and up to 48 kg (105½ lb).

In addition British Powerlifting Championships are staged for juniors, under twenty-threes and seniors. British universities hold annual championships on both forms of lifting.

For the disabled, British Championships are held for paraplegics on the modified Press on Bench. Those who qualify may proceed to the Paraplegic Games section of the Commonwealth Games and the Olympic Games. Chapter 14 gives details of lifting for the disabled.

Incentive Schemes

As well as taking part in the various championships, or breaking records, British lifters have the opportunity to avail themselves of certain incentive schemes. Here, the lifters compete with themselves or against realistic targets. They provide an important source of self-satisfaction and motivation. The popular schemes are outlined below.

Schoolboys' Weight-training and Lifting Awards

This scheme is devised to act as an incentive for schoolboys who start weight-training and then progress to weightlifting. The examination may be carried out by the boy's usual teacher or coach. Free certificates are awarded for the three different grades. Badges, corresponding to the different schoolboy grades, may be purchased. The three awards are:

Bronze Award This is an inducement for beginners. To qualify, a boy must have practised weight-training regularly to the satisfaction of his teacher or coach for not less than six weeks.

Silver Award To qualify for this, a boy must successfully lift a total of at least one and one-third his bodyweight on the two Olympic lifts. These lifts are described in Chapters 5 and 6.

Gold Award This is a much higher standard than the Silver Award. The total for the Olympic lifts must equal at least double the boy's own bodyweight.

Certificates of Merit

Official recognition for performances at different bodyweight levels for seniors and juniors can be granted by means of the Certificates of Merit scheme. Certificates at first-, second- and third-class levels can be obtained on any of the official thirty-two lifts. The scheme is devised as a progressive method of attaining all-round weightlifting proficiency and for the lifter who does not wish to specialize. There is a Novice Certificate of Merit Scheme on either the Olympic lifts or power lifts for those who have never gained a gold, silver or bronze medal awarded by B.A.W.L.A. or who do not hold and have never held a national record.

B.A.W.L.A. Grading and Incentive Scheme

There is a scheme for those who wish to have recognition of their totals on the Olympic lifts or the power lifts. This employs a colour grading method as used in judo. The colours start at yellow, moving progressively to orange, green, blue, brown, black and finally to the much coveted bronze, silver and gold awards. For each colour grade there are three sub-divisions of one, two and three. Thus beginners usually enter at yellow three grade and work upward.

All the categories, with corresponding poundages, are tabulated in the handbook of the governing body. It should be noted that lifters can qualify for these certificates only before a qualified referee.

Two General Principles I

Weight-training: A Prerequisite to Lifting

After suitable preparation, many young weight-trainers are attracted towards the official lifts. Not only do they appreciate weight-training as a worthwhile physical activity but they often wish to practise the sport of weightlifting. It is natural for them to want to apply their strength in an accepted way in order to measure their performance. Also, the acquisition and mastery of a skill appeals to a number of young lifters. A number of boys join weightlifting clubs while still at school; some join clubs when they leave school. Others like to have a competitive sport while they continue full-time education. But it is essential that they receive correct early guidance and support. Also, it is important for these young people, usually in their mid-teens, to have benefited from a sound basic physical education programme which, among other things, ensures that they have sufficient organic vigour and a thirst for the accomplishment of satisfying movement, which can be recreative as well as competitive.

Weight-training and the sport of weightlifting can have definite carry-over value. The competitive aspects are graded for schoolboys and juniors, while numerous colleges and universities have clubs where regular training or the attainment of awards can take place. In addition, the universities stage yearly championships. There are categories for the under twenty-threes as well as for seniors. There are incentive schemes related to differences in age and graded according to bodyweight for all levels of performance. The attainment of the lowest award or even modest success in a competition can bring satisfaction, which in turn fosters the individual's development.

As previously indicated, careful conditioning and a groundwork of graded weight-training exercises are prerequisites to actual lifting. Physical fitness and systematic training form a basis for more arduous activity in the future. This groundwork takes time to establish, and in the best interests of young people it must not be hurried since magical results cannot be expected overnight. Regular training workouts, at least three times a week, have been found to produce satisfactory results. It should be pointed out that training should never be carried out to the point of undue fatigue of the whole body and the nervous system. Training can be recreative and arranged so as to bring about gradual increases in strength and development. After at least a year of careful training, lifting techniques *per se* can be acquired.

To help the necessary balance and co-ordination of complex lifting movements, suitable skills exercises have to be introduced. Most of these exercises are sectional, with elements in common with the techniques they are designed to assist. This enables the best possible transfer of training to occur. Such exercises help in the development of the correct neuromuscular pathways. They are called 'assistance exercises' and will be described in detail later in this book. On some of the exercises, the progressive overload can be stepped up. But the execution of lifts with maximum poundage should occur infrequently. The teacher or coach has to judge this very carefully, keeping poundages light until capabilities are known. Irregularity of working out is not good training; nor is the prolonged use of very heavy weights. Safety precautions must be taught, and it must be realized that correct technique takes time to establish. Good standards invariably follow after two or three years of such training. Awards, incentive schemes and competitions can stimulate young men to higher targets, besides reinforcing interest which can last. Later, suitable programmes, methods and precautions will be described in detail.

Personal Requirements

There are many personal requirements or qualities necessary in order to become a really successful weightlifter. Because man is a 'mind-body unity' there are psychological as well as physical areas which have to be identified, but they all relate to the whole person. The psychological areas will be covered first and will be followed by the more obvious athletic and physical areas.

Dedication

Because the groundwork of progressive exercises necessary for the development of a successful lifter takes time to establish, and also because the arduous training which follows can take years before real success is experienced, it is clear that dedication is an important personal requirement for a lifter. The hard work and regular training needed to develop the muscular and organic systems has to be sustained by self-discipline. Sometimes training plateaux or setbacks in competition occur. Only the sort of self-discipline which engenders determined personal resilience to overcome such obstacles can be effective. In short, a successful lifter needs dedication and self-control if he is to display the physical and mental toughness which are characteristic of top-line lifters. As World and Olympic champion Alexeev (110 kg plus category) puts it: 'Persistent, painstaking, dedicated work is the foundation of good performances.'

Will Power

Will power is necessary for success. Indeed the old-fashioned notion of strength of character applies to weightlifters who desire to win. Negative character traits are not demonstrated by weightlifters of any standing. They have the 'guts' or 'moral fibre', or, put simply, the will to win, whether it be in competition or establishing a personal record. Perseverance is an important character trait for lifters. It has to do with being honest with oneself; for example in recognizing a particular weakness such as poor pulling power and taking positive steps, sometimes long-term, to overcome that deficiency. Here the role of the teacher or coach is to help identify any weakness and then to work positively with his pupil to remedy the problem, which must be evaluated periodically. In broad terms, the coach must help his lifter to meet difficulties squarely, and not to make excuses about the issue; this applies at all levels.

Concentration

The ability to concentrate on the lift or a hard part of training is an asset. Careful conditioning can help where concentration is suspect. There are many things going on when lifting, some are related to the task in hand, while others are not. The latter can be distractions such as noise or pressure during competition. Tommy Kono (U.S.A.), winner of three Olympic weightlifting medals, had marvellous powers of concentration: when about to lift, he appeared to be thinking deeply while totally detached from external stresses.

Courage

Fear can inhibit performance. It is quite plain that the lifting of a heavy barbell, or performing a new skill for the first time, requires courage. Without courage a lifter can never make the grade. However, good training, coaching and encouragement and confidence in one's ability can help to remove fear. Steinhouse and Ikai, authorities on strength, demonstrated that when psychological inhibitions were removed, strength levels could be raised significantly. The coach has to raise the lifter's psychological limits since invariably there is a considerable discrepancy between what the lifter thinks is his maximum and what he is actually capable of. To break through this gap demands great courage, but a good teacher or coach can help to motivate the lifter by using the right phrases, suggesting realistic targets in an appropriate tone of voice, the application of tactile stimulation such as a slap on the hips or elsewhere, and by using other stimuli.

Learning Ability

The ability to learn is another important personal requirement of a lifter. Not only must he learn to apply strength in a given technique, but also he should acquire a positive attitude towards training and competition. Although mistakes are made, he can benefit from experience and accept that they can be corrected. Skill is a learned ability.

Physical Fitness

In a broad sense, physical fitness may be defined as 'the capacity of an individual to perform work'. Fleishman (1964) uses the term 'physical fitness' to refer to 'the functional capacity of individuals to perform certain kinds of tasks requiring muscular activity'. Physical fitness in weightlifting has to do with excellence in that sport, and the ability to cope with the heavy work and stress in weightlifting competition and its related training. It is concerned with skill training and conditioning. Lifting needs a different kind of fitness to that required by sportsmen such as footballers, swimmers, fencers and so forth. Each of these sports has its own fitness requirements. Likewise, weightlifting has its own specific requirements; these differ between Olympic weightlifters and powerlifters. The specific fitness parameters do not fall into discrete, watertight compartments.

The following fitness factors are of concern to lifters and their coaches.

Muscular Power

Mechanically, power is the rate of doing work. Morgan and Adamson (1957) contend that 'power shows itself in the ability to propel one's own body or some other object rapidly through space'. In Olympic weightlifting it is the combination of speed and strength to produce fast weightlifting movements and here the term 'explosive power' is appropriate. With heavy 'powerlifting', power is more dependent on strength than on speed. Power is consequent upon the tension developed in muscles when moving the levers of the body, the range through which muscles act on the levers, and the rate at which the action occurs. However, lifting ability is dependent on the way power is applied.

Muscular Strength

Strength is the capacity to overcome resistance in a single muscular effort. Clark (1957) refers to strength as 'the amount of tension a muscle can apply in a single maximum contraction'. Adamson (1963) defines strength as 'the ultimate capacity of a muscle to exert tension'. These notions of strength are concerned with pure, rather than applied, muscular strength as seen in Olympic weightlifting and powerlifting. Weightlifters require very strong muscular frames. They must be capable of applying great pulling and pushing strength, or dynamic strength; and applying strength of a static nature where weights are momentarily held in certain positions during and at the finish of a lift. This involves the ability to switch from one type of muscular exertion to another.

Muscular Endurance

During training and actual lifting, muscles have to continue working without fatigue. In weightlifting proper, we are concerned with heavy performances carried out in a matter of a few seconds. In training for weightlifting, performances of continuous localized activity are necessary. In both of these cases muscular fatigue may occur. This demands local muscular endurance which meets additional work from the major muscles responsible for the movement in question. Muscular endurance has been defined as 'the quality which enables muscles to maintain contractions or a contraction in conditions of fatigue, or the ability to continue and postpone and tolerate fatigue' (Sedgwick (1962)).

Muscular endurance depends on training, which improves circulatory processes by increasing capillarity. In addition the muscles become adapted to work and can tolerate conditions of fatigue. In weightlifting increased muscular endurance facilitates increased toleration of oxygen debt. Powerlifters handle very heavy weights both in competition and in training—they require moderate local muscular endurance. Those practising the fast lifts require a high level of muscular endurance. Both types of lifters have to recover between lifts in competition or between exercises in training.

Cardiovascular Endurance

For better weightlifting performances and faster recovery between lifts or exercises, efficient cardiac, vascular and capillary actions are required. Such efficiency involves the heart, lungs, arterial system and capillaries so as to supply oxygen to the working muscles. Whereas muscular endurance is local, cardiovascular endurance is general. A more efficient heart pumps more blood with fewer beats, and heart rate, blood pressure and cardiovascular recovery return much sooner to resting levels than is the case with an inefficient, untrained cardiovascular system.

In recent years cardiovascular training has become more fashionable among Olympic lifters. Such lifters now incorporate jogging, short bursts of interval running, circuit training and high-repetition work with weights in their programmes. Increased performances have resulted.

NEUROMUSCULAR CO-ORDINATION

Balance, timing, speed of movement, kinaesthetic sense, agility and flexibility are some of the important qualities a lifter needs in order to establish the co-ordinated neuromuscular pathways necessary for the development of good technique. In Olympic weightlifting more athletic ability is required than in powerlifting. However, the powerlifter still needs co-ordination and a certain amount of flexibility and timing. In the former case, skill training is quite complex. In the latter it is less complicated but nevertheless important, and must not be devalued since special powerlifting skills in their own right have to be acquired.

FLEXIBILITY

Flexibility refers to joint mobility or range of movement at a joint. It has been shown to be a factor in physical fitness and sports ability (Cureton (1941); Kraus (1954)). Efficient execution of the fast lifts necessitates adequate range of movement at certain principal joints. In particular, mobility of the ankles, hips, shoulders and knees is important. Flexibility work forms part of a weightlifter's training: free exercises, partner-assisted exercises and exercises with barbells and other apparatus are used. In order to counteract short ligaments, muscles and fascia, and other restrictions to movement, the joint is taken to the point of maximum flexibility and then taken a little beyond this point. Slow pressure to produce maximum stretch, rather than a jerk, is required. Flexibility work is usually incorporated into the end of a training session because then the muscles are warm and often shorter. Also, mobility work may be included near the end of the warm-up.

Tests

In recent years screenings, followed by regular fitness tests, have been administered to weightlifters. These are based on the following.

1. Explosive power: tested by vertical and broad jumps.
2. Speed: tested by 50–60 m sprints.
3. Strength: tested by barbells or dynamometers.
4. Cardiovascular endurance: tested by the Harvard step test or suitable oxygen uptake tests.
5. Flexibility: tested by goniometers or special tests.

Test details may be found in suitable physical education books on physical fitness or tests and measurements.

Three General Principles II

Further Strength Considerations

A high degree of muscular strength is required by weightlifters. But the sort of strength seen in the action of Olympic lifters differs from that of powerlifters. Not only are the movements different, but they are performed at different speeds. Furthermore, a different kind of kinaesthetic sense appears to be necessary for Olympic weightlifting. Also, the motivating forces and anxieties involved appear to be of a different nature. All of this suggests that strength is specific to the type of lifting in question.

In competitive lifting of any kind, the lifter must try to induce his entire energy potential into the execution of the lift. This involves psychical as well as energy, muscular, neurological and tactical factors. However, the fundamental factor is the transformation of energy into action. This action can be brought about only by mechanisms leading up to the development of tension in muscles. In competition, the work of the muscles is carried out in one or more of the following ways: with maximum weight; with maximum speed; and with maximum precision. The first two requirements involve muscular strength and muscular endurance in variable proportions, while the third is concerned with neuromuscular co-ordination.

Muscles create movement. Through the ability of motor units to contract, muscles produce strength which can act on their own body masses and other resistances such as weights to change states of both rest and motion. Muscular strength is a complex notion, for it must take into account speed of contraction, duration of work, degree of muscular tension and other qualities. In order to simplify highly complicated physical and physiological considerations, the following qualities which are employed to improve the work capabilities of lifters will be used: strength, speed and weight.

Superimposed on these are the lifter's inherited characteristics, which condition his adaptability to lifting training and competitive performance. There are fixed limits which are genetically based. This explains why similar training systems produce individual results which are vastly different. It has been suggested, for example, that Asian lifters perform relatively better on the Snatch than the Clean and Jerk because of the short arms which they have inherited. It is an advantage in weightlifting to be endowed with an athletic or mesomorphic physique. But not all top lifters are mesomorphs.

Lifters who lack speed and kinaesthetic perception will find the mastery of the skills of the classic lifts very difficult. However, if they are physically strong, they may do well on the power lifts. But training is a powerful determinant of lifting efficiency. Without proper and sustained training, success in Olympic lifting or powerlifting is unlikely.

Strengthening for lifters necessitates performing exercises which bring about adequate degrees of tension in the muscles, with the intensity of contraction dependent upon various stimuli and the amount of weight on the bar. De Lorme and Watkins (1951) demonstrated that when muscles work against a resistance, carefully chosen and progressively graded, an increase in strength occurs. This is the well-known 'overload' or 'progressive resistance exercise' principle. According to Walters (1958), the application of the overload principle will increase muscular strength, size (hypertrophy) and endurance, which result from an increase in the intensity of work performed in a given time unit. Relatively low exercise repetitions result in an increase in strength, whereas relatively high repetitions increase endurance.

Coaches should note that when young lifters and novices train for strength, they should take into account repetitions, systematic working, gradual increase in the weights used, and preparatory work by way of warming-up, physical fitness and special exercises. It cannot be overemphasized that novices must not use weights which are too heavy before they have developed an adequate physical foundation. In the initial stages of training, beginners use up to approximately 50 and 65 per cent of their bodyweight as the weight of the barbell for training on the Snatch and the Clean and Jerk, respectively.

More experienced lifters sometimes use maximum training loads; at other times they use light or medium loads. Much of the training intensity is within the range of 60 to 90 per cent of maximum. Speed and full-range movements are often used, depending upon the stage of training. Sometimes they exert great muscular tension in static positions, which has been referred to as 'isometric' contraction training. Later in this book will be found detailed training methods, describing 'strength build-up' phases and tapering-off methods.

Strength training requires an appropriate diet, both in quality and quantity. Diet provides the energy necessary for training and competition as well as for health. According to Jokl (1972), better nutrition has engendered 'major demonstrable performance improvements in many sports, for example in basketball and weightlifting'. A high-calorie diet, rich in protein, together with all the ingredients of a varied and well-balanced diet is advocated. Lifters sometimes use food supplements such as multivitamin tablets and wheat germ oil. Lifters are concerned with bodyweight and diet is a factor in this.

Strength training must be complemented by adequate rest, of both a passive and active nature. Sufficient sleep must be obtained by lifters. Most of them require a minimum of eight hours nightly. Also rest pauses during training and careful spacing of workouts are important to ensure full recovery. Rest is necessary to overcome inefficiency due to fatigue. The use of fairly light weights (less than 60 per cent of maximum) as a form of 'active rest' is sometimes used when fatigue persists.

Olympic Lifts

Although lifters in the 110 kg plus class lift the heaviest weights in both the Snatch and the Clean and Jerk, their relative strength is not as great as that of lighter weightlifters .

In the 1973 World Championships, Nassiri of Iran in the 52 kg class had a strength–bodyweight ratio of 4·6 : 1 as compared with 2·8 : 1 for Alexeev of the U.S.S.R. in the 110 kg plus category. Each of the 159 lifters who made totals at these Championships jerked considerably more than they snatched.

Power Lifts

Based on the three-lift power totals, the lighter bodyweight categories of lifters have greater relative strength–bodyweight ratios when compared with superheavyweights.

In the 1973 World Powerlifting Championships, McKenzie of Great Britain in the 56 kg class had a strength–bodyweight ratio of 9·6 : 1 as compared with 6·6 : 1 for Reidhoudt of the U.S.A. in the 110 kg plus category.

Most of the forty-eight lifters who registered totals at the 1973 World Powerlifting Championships held at Harrisburg, U.S.A., lifted more in the Dead Lift than in the Deep Knees' Bend (Squat), although Reidhoudt squatted 12½ per cent more than he dead lifted. In every case, the powerlifters squatted and dead lifted more than they bench pressed.

Basic Mechanical Principles

It is important that teachers and pupils of weightlifting understand some of the basic mechanical principles if they are to appreciate the scientific basis of lifting movements. The following mechanical concepts and related terms should help.

Force

A force is a push or a pull produced by the action of one body on another. In weightlifting this occurs when muscles contract to exert strength which is a tension of the muscles (denoted by P). The force of gravity (G) has to be contended with. Weights held high push down on a lifter, tending to compress or collapse him; the lifter has to resist this pressure. For this reason coaches very often call out to lifters 'resist'. When pulling with straight arms in lifting, the weight of the bar tends to stretch the arm muscles which are in tension. In lifting, many movements at joints are involved, therefore a sequential process of forces, together with careful timing is involved. Typically in pulling a weight off the floor, the large muscles of the thighs and hips are used first. This movement is relatively slow in the Dead Lift but quite fast in the Snatch and Clean. Then the muscles of the back are brought into operation, followed by the calves, shoulder elevators, arms and wrists. When well-timed, this brings about an efficient sequence of movement.

Weight

A lifter, or barbell, or other object consists of mass. The force of gravity acting on an object's mass is known as the weight of that object, and pulls downward towards the ground.

Centre of Gravity

The point at which the weight of a body is said to act is known as the centre of gravity (C of G). In lifting we are concerned with the centres of gravity of both the lifter and the barbell. In most lifts the relative position of these is in the same vertical line.

Gravity Line

The gravity line of any object is an imaginary vertical line which passes through its C of G. A plumb line attached to the C of G of an object shows its gravity line. In most lifts the gravity lines of the lifter and the bar are kept close together.

Lever

A lever is a rigid bar which turns about a given point, called a fulcrum. In the human body the bones are levers: for example, moving about the knee joint we have the thigh and shin bones. Fulcra are found at the joints: for example, the ankle, knee and shoulder joints.

Moment of Force

The turning effect of a force about an axis is known as a moment of a force. In the human body movement takes place at joints because the muscles, which are attached to the bones or levers, contract, pulling on the bone and causing it to turn. Since movement at several joints is necessary in lifting, we are concerned with the combined effect of movements. Moreover, the same moment may be felt at several places.

POWER
The rate of supplying energy, or work rate, is known as power. The product of force and velocity is the dynamic aspect of power.

IMPULSE
This is the concept of a force acting during a very short time. For a constant force, impulse is found by multiplying the force (strength) by the time during which the force acts. It is equal to its change of momentum.

CLASSES OF LEVERS
Depending upon the positions of the fulcrum (F), the point of application of force or muscle tension (P) and the point where the weight or resistance acts (W), we have three possible combinations or classes of levers.

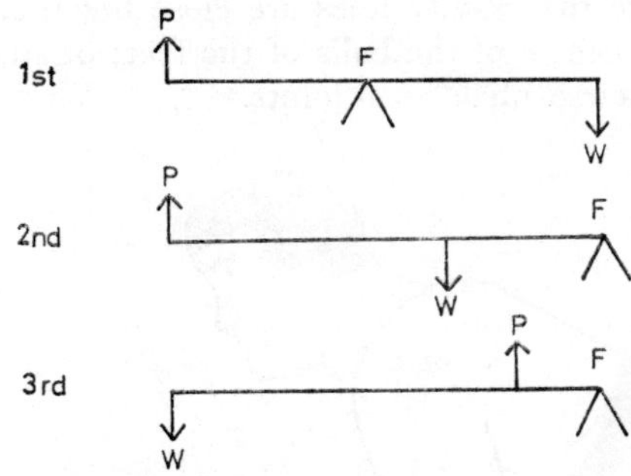

FIGURE 1. Classes of lever

In lifting we are concerned mainly with muscles, bones and joints which are third-class systems of levers. These are designed for speed rather than strength. At the conclusion of a pull in the Snatch or Clean, the elbows bend sideways in a W–P–F situation, which is a third-class lever system.

POWER AND WEIGHT ARMS
The horizontal distance between P and F is known as the power arm (PA). The horizontal distance between W and F is known as the weight arm (WA). The length of bones and points of insertion of muscles are important determinants of applied muscle strength.

The relationship for static contractions, such as the lifter has to adopt at the conclusion of a lift, is shown by the simple formula:

$$\text{Power} \times \text{Power Arm} = \text{Weight} \times \text{Weight Arm}$$

or

$$P \times PA = W \times WA$$

For dynamic lifting to get a weight moving upward:

$$P \times PA > W \times WA$$

This is because the force exerted by the muscles must overcome the total weight and other forms of resistance. The muscles have to work against gravity to accelerate the mass of the weight as well as the lifter's body.

Balance

Balance or equilibrium is essential for a lifter, whether he is in a static or dynamic position. Throughout any lift he is affected by the force of gravity. The following conditions apply to a lifter if he is to be balanced.

1. Both the C of G of the lifter and the bar must be above some point of his base; as shown in Figure 2, which illustrates the 'get set' position. Here the gravity lines are close together or coincide to pass over the centre of the balls of the feet; or anatomically, over the first metatarso-phalangeal joints.

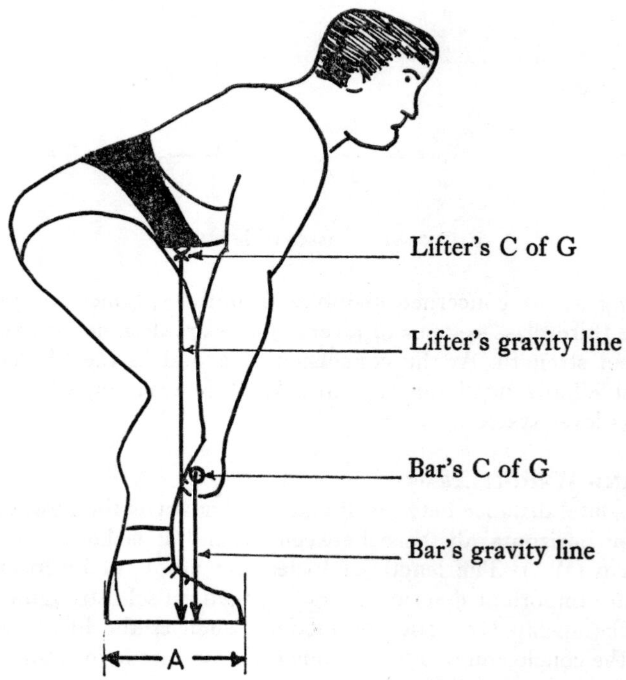

FIGURE 2. The mechanically balanced 'get set' position
(A represents the width of the lifter's base)

2. The larger the base of the lifter, the steadier is his balance. In Plate 16 the split Clean is more stable than the pulling position.
3. The heavier the weight of the lifter and barbell, the more stable should be his balance.
4. Balance depends on the height of the combined Cs of G. So a lifter with a heavy weight overhead has to control his balance carefully. Tall lifters with long arms often find it difficult to control weights overhead.
5. If the combined gravity lines of the lifter and barbell are near the edge of the base of support, he is near to losing his balance.
6. A lifter needs a good sense of balance, which depends on efficient sensory organs of balance and good kinaesthetic sense. Sensations in muscles, joints, tendons, hands, feet and other areas provide information necessary for this sense of balance. These sensations are affected by fatigue.

Reactive Force

Newton's Law of Reaction states that for every force there is an equal and opposite 'reactive force' or reaction. The supporting surface of the lifting platform provides a force equal to the force placed on it by the lifter. A firm platform enables a lifter to exert force because of the

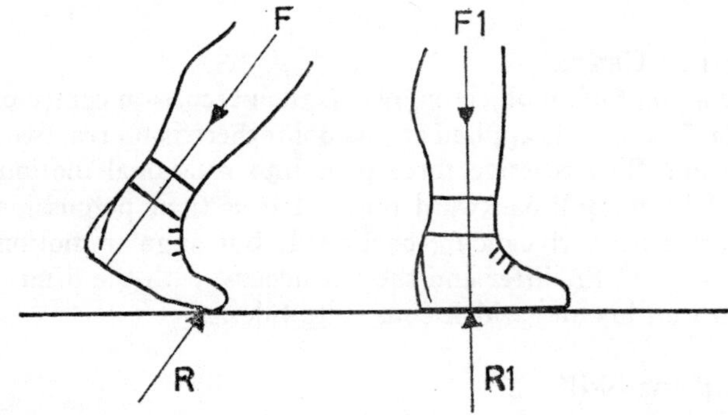

Figure 3. Reactive force acting through a lifter's feet
(R and R1 are the equal and opposite reactive forces to downward forces F and F1)

upward reaction through his feet. The lifter exerts the force downward as does the barbell; and the platform reacts back in the opposite direction. For this reason coaches stress that lifters push with their feet and legs into the platform. In Figure 3, the lifter has to contend with a tendency to slip.

DIRECTION OF APPLICATION OF FORCE

In lifts such as the Jerk or Press on Bench, the aim is to finish with the weight on locked arms directly over the shoulder joints. If the weight is driven forward it may be lost. The weight has to move along the correct path towards the finishing position. This necessitates a correct direction of application of muscular force.

INERTIA

Body masses resist a change of position or motion unless acted upon by an external force. Lifters have to overcome the inertia of the barbell as well as gravity when lifting it from the platform. Once in motion the bar tends to retain velocity, apart from the pull of gravity which decelerates it. Where possible, the action has to be done quickly.

LINEAR AND ANGULAR MOTION

The ideal way to lift a bar from the platform is to get it to travel in a straight line, or in linear motion. In the early stages of the pull for the Snatch or Clean, the hips move in linear fashion. In order to do this the thighs and shins move with angular motion. Different parts of the body move in various complicated manners, involving both linear and angular motion. At the conclusion of the pull in the classic lifts, control of the angular velocity of the lifter's back, which is his longest lever, is important.

PERCUSSION CENTRE

There is a point of an object known as the percussion centre or centre of inertia. If a force is applied at this point there is no reactive force at the fulcrum. The reactive force goes into rotational motion. Some advanced lifters pull backward on the bar at their percussion centre height without overbalancing backward; but angular motion of the whole system of the lifter and the bar occurs, with the lifter pushing downward on his toes which constitute fulcra.

Weightlifting Skill

NEUROLOGICAL POINTS

Effective weightlifting demands highly developed motor skill, which in turn requires more than strength, speed or endurance. It requires a functional integrity of the nervous system. Weightlifting skill is based on co-ordinated muscular activity, with a high degree of precision and control. Although weightlifting skill tends to develop slowly, it is not easily lost. According to Russian research, movement patterns with top weights are not the same as those with lighter weights. Lifting heavy weights with good technique is characterized by a highly developed kinaesthetic sense, whereby the lifter has to be acutely conscious of his muscular movement, as well as the position of his body, limbs and barbell. The heavier the weight, the keener must be this perception.

Skill and Learning

Motor skill can be regarded as a factor in the level of performance of lifting. Knapp (1963), has defined skill as 'the learned ability to bring about predetermined results with maximum certainty, often with a minimum outlay of time or energy, or both'. This definition is an inclusive one which covers the main features of weightlifting skill, stressing learning. Although neuromuscular development, endurance and speed are not learned, skill is. In lifting techniques, the young lifter has to spend time learning mechanically sound and efficient movement patterns. He has to practise assiduously and repetitively to produce conditioned reflexes until they are automatic.

There are various ways of learning. In lifting, direct instruction methods are often used. Trial-and-error methods do occur, but generally are not advocated for safety reasons and the fact that they can lead to incorrect responses. Learning by imitation from good models such as coaches or visual aids is used a good deal. Brief, clear explanations accompany visual impressions so as to make it quite plain what are the main aims of a movement. Correction of faults is a must, with immediate feedback. Correct practice should be positively reinforced with appropriate rewards such as praise and the knowledge and satisfaction that a correct movement has been achieved. The fast lifts are complex and their mastery may become a long-term process. Not only has the coach to sustain the lifter in this process, but he has to do so at later stages, when technique has to be modified.

Mental rehearsal of correct movement patterns seems to help lifters with good visual imagery, but it is important that lifters have the sense to know what is going on and what are the coaching objectives.

Skills Coaching Advice

With beginners, it has been empirically found that a simple warm-up should precede skills sessions. As a start some general cardiovascular work to step up the circulatory and respiratory processes should be included. Then follow full-range flexibility exercises related to the movements to be practised. Shadow lifting with a bar only or with a barbell with wooden weights comes next. At all times the weights should be kept light enough to allow the lifter to get the correct feel of the movement. Early objectives in teaching beginners are the attainment of precision, with moderate speed. Later on, when the neuromuscular responses become statisfactorily established, speed of movement can be increased. Attention must be paid to the correction of major faults. In general, more complicated movements are taught in phases or parts. Later they are blended into the whole movement, which is subject to correction by focusing on one important coaching feature at a time. Simple lifts are practised as whole movements. The young lifter should not have to worry about the actual weight on the bar. His attention should be fixed on producing acceptable movement patterns, or parts of those movements. Sessions should finish with a few minutes of moderate exercise consisting of massive free movements and jogging so as to aid the oxidization of fatigue products in the body.

More advanced work includes assistance exercises and other sectional practices with progressively heavier weights. This facilitates good technique with heavy weights. Since transfer of training is highly specific, these exercises must have elements in common with the lift they are designed to assist. This applies to the intensity, or actual weight, on the bar; but heavy competitive poundages simply cannot be lifted if practice weights are kept light all of the time.

Coaches should aim for positive transfer of training on matters such as correct mechanics, besides speed and how to rescue a lift that may go astray. Attention has to be given to the lowering of the bar and the action to take if a lift cannot be fought and saved. In advanced training, phases or cycles are the components of training programmes. Typical phases include a combined strength and skill phase, followed by a skill phase (with heavy weights) and tapering off.

Coaches must be flexible and ready to adjust to individual susceptibilities which may exist by way of interest, inclination, athletic ability, intelligence, temperament and so forth. One problem is that beginners are more concerned to lift heavy weights before they have acquired good technique. The acquisition of good pulling pathways, well-balanced receiving positions, recovery and control at the end of a lift takes time and patience. In the long-term interests of the lifters it is up to the coach to defer maximum weight at the expense of skill. The rewards come later so faulty habits and attitudes have to be discouraged at the start, since they are difficult to extinguish once they become ingrained.

Pupils must not be mentally or physically fatigued or bored when practising lifting skills. Usually lack of energy accompanies fatigue, thereby thwarting attempts at skilled movement. According to Karonov, the strength and speed stimulators are found in that part of the brain known as the cerebral cortex, between the kinaesthetic and motor cells. Fatigue is accompanied by inhibitory processes in the nervous system which hamper performance in both strength and skill.

Four Making a Start

Adolescents

Teenage boys can start safely with light weight-training exercises provided they are in good health and do not suffer from diseases or injuries of the spine or very bad posture. Boys who have undergone several years of well-rounded physical education programmes in school will have developed physically to a certain extent and may be seen competing in traditional sports as well as practising a wide variety of physical activities.

In any given age group of boys, there will be differences in physique. Some boys in their early teens look like adults, while others look like children. Even the less physically precocious boys of thirteen or fourteen can be introduced to basic weight-training exercises, provided they are correctly taught and the starting weights kept light. The author has seen girl swimmers of eight years of age use light weights to the benefit of their swimming performance and not to their physical detriment.

However, it is not suggested that all young people use weights at that age, but that boys in their second year in secondary education can be introduced safely to weight-training. After all, if they can lift heavy gymnasium apparatus, push in the scrum, participate in athletics, and handle their own bodies, then the use of weights carefully geared to the existing strength of the boys can be approved also. Boys between fourteen and sixteen tend to be dissatisfied with their body images. The motivation to improve their physiques comes at that time.

Weightlifting can be introduced to a boy when he has done progressive weight-training for six to twelve months to ensure a good physical foundation. Forcing with heavy weights is wrong. Skills work with a light barbell is appropriate. In 1947 the American lightweight lifter, Pete George, was National and World champion at sixteen. He was Olympic champion the year after and also won other World Championships. No damage was sustained: in fact he grew heavier, moving from the 67·5 kg to the 75 kg category. Many lifters in their mid-teens can clean and jerk over 135 kg (297½ lb). In most cases they were correctly taught, their programmes carefully supervised, with increases made carefully and gently over a period of time.

In East Germany and Sweden boys learn weightlifting skills at the age of twelve. The weights used are very light. Skill is emphasized: the East Germans claim this is the best age for co-ordination.

In Denmark, a boy may start to train for weightlifting, but he is not granted a licence to take part in competitions until he is fourteen. In Finland, boys start lifting at fourteen, although one of their top lifters, Kailajarvi, started at twelve. In Japan a boy in his early teens may start weightlifting.

Safety Precautions

Safety in the use of weights may be divided into personal and external safety. The general principle to apply is to ensure that all adequate precautions are taken to prevent personal accidents or damage to surroundings. Personal injuries and other accidents are preventable in the majority of cases.

Personal Safety Precautions

Weight-training and lifting can be safe. In a recent massive study conducted in East Germany, injuries in strength sports had a higher incidence in sports other than weightlifting. In the research carried out at the 1966 Children and Youth Games in Berlin, the accident rate in weightlifting had the smallest value among a total of twenty sports. This is ascribed to the careful preparation and the special techniques employed. In particular, the flat-back technique is stressed for personal safety as well as desirable body mechanics.

The British medical profession is concerned with the promotion of proper back management. This is taught in weight-training and lifting so as to preserve the integrity of the intervertebral discs. It has been calculated that loads held safely by the spinal column in a flat-back position can increase sevenfold when the body is bent forward through 70 degrees. There is the danger of uneven wear of the intervertebral discs in this situation. Flat-back (see Chapters 5, 6, 7 and 10) positions should be taught for the 'get set' position, Cleans and Squats, and exercises where a weight is lifted from below the hips. The correct sequencing and use of the extensor muscles of the knees and hips (quadriceps and gluteals) is important when lifting a weight from the floor. The knee and hip joints constitute important mechanical turning points when lifting under load—used correctly a 40 per cent relief on the spinal column can be achieved, according to Munchinger. Correct techniques are described in detail in later chapters. Stress on adductor muscles of the legs is proportional to the deviation from the ideal position in the split. Symmetrical movement emphasizing level hips and shoulders is safe and conducive to bilateral development. It is dangerous to favour one side which laterally tilts the pelvis and shoulders, sometimes with rotation of the spine. The important general point is that mechanically good body positions are safe and should be taught at the beginning and stressed throughout later training.

Attention should be given to the warm-up, which is explained in detail in Chapter 7. To avoid muscle injuries, the whole of the body should be warmed up generally, and specific muscle groups and movement patterns should be covered by appropriate exercises. Unless the internal environment of the training area is perfect with respect to heating and ventilation, track suits must be worn to conserve heat and to avoid local chilling. A moderate to quick tempo of training helps the lifter to keep warm. Standing around for long spells between exercises is undesirable.

Correct observation of the fundamental principles of progressive resistance exercise should be adhered to. Attempting limit poundages too soon is to be deprecated.

Distress can occur if the breathing procedure is wrongly carried out. The correct time to inhale and exhale is given for each lift and exercise described in this book. In the majority of exercises, inhalation occurs as the effort is made, while the exhalation occurs as the weight is returned to the starting position. However, there are examples where this procedure is reversed as in the case of movements where the thorax is fixed under the pressure of the weight. Here the blood flow back to the heart is impaired. This can cause dizziness or even blackouts. This is known as the Valsalva phenomenon and is consistent with straining rather than training. In practice, the breathing for Squats, abdominal exercises, Bench Presses and related exercises and Cleans should be carefully carried out if distress is to be averted.

In addition to squatting, hyperventilation or overbreathing can also occur when cleaning a heavy weight. Sometimes a lifter experiences a blackout; recovery is quick and may be assisted by the use of smelling salts. For the few who have experienced such blackouts, doctors recommend that hyperventilation be avoided, squatting should be brief, and that the barbell is raised as quickly as possible to a position where it can be supported while normal breathing is resumed.

It is clear that persons with abnormalities of the respiratory or circulatory systems should not practise heavy weightlifting or strenuous weight-training.

External Safety Precautions

Equipment should be suitable, well made and maintained, and carefully laid out; barbell and dumb-bell collars kept tight; and apparatus kept secure. Manual handling and transport of apparatus should be executed carefully and in accordance with safe mechanical principles. Back should be kept flat, chin kept in and a firm grip used. The floor of the exercise area should be firm and level. Preferably, it should be protected and be of the non-skid variety. Polished wooden floors are unsuitable. The apparatus and groups should be arranged so that there is plenty of elbow room: crowding can lead to accidents. Orderly movement procedure and safe organization of the training area prevent accidents.

Certain exercises need the cooperation of others. Inexperienced persons should not train alone. Approved methods of standing in should be practised. There should be no draughts in the gymnasium or other training areas since they cause local cooling as sweat evaporates thereby creating conditions predisposing to muscle injuries. For the same reason, the body should be kept covered with a track suit even though a lifter may sweat profusely.

Equipment

As will be seen from the illustrations in this book, various pieces of equipment are used in weight-training and lifting. Enumerated in the following section are some of the more common items.

Barbell In its basic form this is simply a steel bar 152–83 cm (5–6 ft) long and weighing approximately 7·5 kg (16½ lb). Weights are attached to its ends. They are secured by two fixed and two movable collars for safety. Sometimes a sleeve is fitted. The bar or sleeve is usually knurled to ensure firmness of grip. The plain barbell is commonly used for weight-training. Depending on its length a barbell can be loaded from 7·5 kg (16½ lb) to 230 kg (507 lb) or more in any multiple of 1·25 kg (2¾ lb).

International Barbell This is a high-grade engineering product used for weightlifting and powerlifting competitions and related training purposes. It consists of a high-tensile steel bar. At each end is a large-diameter steel sleeve which is fitted with bearings to enable it to revolve freely around the bar. The sleeves are kept in place with fixed collars. Disc weights can be slipped on to the sleeves of the barbell. Quick-release collars hold the weights on to the sleeves. The barbell and collars together weigh 25 kg (55 lb).

The I.W.F.'s specifications for the international pattern barbell are:

a. Distance between the inside collars: 131 cm (51$\frac{9}{16}$ in) minimum.
b. Width of the inside collars, including the collar on the sleeve: 20 mm ($\frac{25}{32}$ in) minimum, 40 mm (1$\frac{9}{16}$ in) maximum.
c. Total length outside the sleeves: 2·20 m (7 ft 2¾ in) maximum.
d. Diameter of the bar: 28 mm (1$\frac{5}{64}$ in).
e. Diameter of the sleeve: 50 mm (1$\frac{31}{32}$ in) minimum, 55 mm (2$\frac{5}{32}$ in) maximum.

Disc Weights Flat circular weights of iron or steel are loaded on to barbells according to the desired weight. On the international barbell the range is: 1·25 kg (2¾ lb); 2·5 kg (5½ lb); 5 kg (11 lb); 10 kg (22 lb);

15 kg (33 lb); 20 kg (44 lb)—which must be coloured blue; 25 kg (55 lb)—which must be coloured red; and 50 kg (110 lb)—which must be coloured green. Other types of barbell have a similar range of weights sometimes with discs of 50 kg (110 lb). Some disc weights are rubber-coated for more agreeable acoustics and safeguarding of the platform.

Platform Competition lifts are carried out on a strong wooden platform measuring 4 m (13 ft 1½ in) square.

Dumb-bells A pair of dumb-bells consists of two steel rods up to 45·6 cm (18 in) long, with a short revolving sleeve and collars with screws for securing the weights to the dumb-bell bars. The weight of a dumb-bell can be altered from 2·5 kg (5½ lb) to any multiple of 1·25 kg (2¾ lb) up to 50 kg (110 lb) or more. Preferably they should be loaded with discs having rounded edges. Sometimes solid dumb-bells of fixed weights are used.

Swingbell This is a centrally loaded dumb-bell used for special weight-training exercises.

Squat Stands Squat stands are used for supporting heavy weights for such exercises as Squats or Jerks. They save the lifter the trouble of having to lift the weight from the floor. They consist of fixed, strong, vertical steel tubes fastened to substantial bases for stability. Inside the fixed members are adjustable steel bars with V-shaped supports at the top for holding the barbell. Strong, steel pins fix into holes in the adjustable bars at the desired height.

Flat Bench The flat bench is used for performing exercises and lifts when lying on the back. Usually it consists of a steel frame and legs with a firm wooden top. For competitive bench pressing and other lifts, it should conform to the specification of the I.P.F., described in Chapter 10. (See Appendix for dimensions of the bench used by paraplegic lifters.)

Inclined Bench The inclined bench is similar to the flat bench but it has a top which is hinged about 30·4 mm (12 in) from one end, so that it can be moved from the horizontal through any angle to the vertical. At the desired angle the safety strut should be firmly locked into place.

Abdominal Board This is a sloping board some 2 m (6 ft 6 in) long adjustable from the horizontal to 45 degrees from the floor. At the lower end it touches the floor while at the higher end it rests on two strong legs. At the higher end is a strap for securing the feet. In use, due to increased leverage, a stronger than usual effect results when performing abdominal exercises.

Overhead Rack Typically this training device consists of two H-shaped members set about 130 cm (4 ft 3¼ in) apart and securely fastened to the floor and ceiling. The horizontal parts and adjustable bars fit into holes spaced at regular intervals in the uprights. These bars support the barbell close to the inside collars. Great weights can be moved safely through a short range or supported isometrically. The overhead rack is used to strengthen a lifter in overhead movements.

Wrist Roller The wrist roller consists of a short wooden handle mounted at each end into blocks fitted with bearings to reduce friction. In turn these are mounted on substantial uprights or to the wall. One end of strong rope or steel cable is fastened to the centre of the handle or roller; weights are attached to the other end of the rope. The grip is strengthened by winding the roller, which causes the rope to wind around it thereby lifting the weights off the floor.

Lifting Blocks Pairs of lifting blocks enable the barbell to be placed above platform level for pulling exercises. They may be of fixed height or adjustable.

Lifting Straps Lifting straps are training aids used for lifting heavy weights off the floor. They are used when the grip is tired or when it is wished to lift heavier weights than usual. Each strap is made of strong webbing or similar material. In use the hand fits through the loop which rests on the back of the wrist. The remainder of the strap is wrapped around the bar with a half-hitch, and the palm and fingers encircle the strap and bar.

Other Equipment Specialized training machines such as a calf machine, quadriceps exerciser, wall pulley, 'multi-gym', leg-press machine and back-extension machine may be used from time to time for special effects.

Personal Kit

To start with, any existing clothing such as a football shirt and shorts may be used. Plimsolls and a track suit should be acquired as soon as possible. When training progresses to lifting for awards or some form of competition, the correct costume must be worn. This consists of a type of leotard under which is worn a support such as neatly fitting trunks. Jock-straps are not permissible under the rules. An alternative type of costume consists of a vest with short sleeves, trunks and approved support. A vest or T-shirt may be worn under the costume: it may have short sleeves which must not extend further than half-way on the upper arms, and it must be collarless.

A pair of lifting boots should be acquired if a lifter becomes serious. They should be comfortable, neither too tight nor too loose, and should not cramp the toes. Leather boots fitted with tarsal straps and non-slip soles are preferable. The toes should curve gently and be neither too pointed, nor too square. The soles should not project too far from the uppers.

A belt is optional in competition, but its use for that purpose and for training is recommended because it supports the whole of the trunk. One made of supple, good-quality leather and which does not pinch the sides of the waist is recommended. The buckle should be strong and securely fastened to the belt.

Basic Terminology

The following terms are commonly used by lifters and will be used throughout this book.

Repetitions The number of times an exercise is repeated before stopping is called the repetitions of that exercise, or 'reps' for short.

Set A group of repetitions of a single exercise is known as a set. Usually one or more sets of an exercise are performed. Five sets of five repetitions may be written in abbreviated form: 5 sets × 5 reps, or merely 5 × 5.

Schedule The schedule is the list of all the exercises used in a training session or workout. It tabulates the order of these exercises, the number of sets and the number of repetitions used. The duration of the schedule is the total time the training period takes.

Load There are various sizes of training load, namely light, medium and heavy. The load has two components known as tonnage and intensity.

Tonnage This is the total weight lifted in a workout, calculated by multiplying the average weights lifted by the total number of repetitions. It is synonymous with the term 'load volume'. It is expressed in tonnes or 1,000 kg (2,200 lb): for example, a 15 tonne training period involves a sum total of weight lifted of 15,000 kg (33,000 lb). Tonnage and the number of lifts performed have a correlation coefficient of + 0·96.

Intensity This is the actual weight of the barbell in kilogrammes. In training, the intensity is varied. It is expressed as a percentage of the best lift: for example, heavy intensity refers to 90 per cent or more of the best performance on a particular lift.

Average Intensity This is calculated by dividing tonnage by the total number of repetitions.

'Active Rest' 'Active rest' consists of activity which helps to remove fatigue. In certain instances it will improve a lifter's efficiency more than passive rest. Heavy training loads cannot be kept up indefinitely and must be balanced with medium loads for maintaining fitness and light loads for recovery purposes or 'active rest'. Examples of 'active rest' are: very light or non-lifting movements during 'rest' weeks; exercising a different part of the body after the main part of a workout—for example, using Bench Presses after training on the Clean or Squat; and reducing the training load during a 'light' period after a 'heavy' period.

Rest Pause This is the recuperation interval between sets or single lifts. Rest pauses constitute the greater part of the schedule's duration which varies from twenty minutes to three hours.
Technique The specific style or form of skilled movement used in the execution of a lift is known as technique. Examples of weightlifting and powerlifting techniques are the split Snatch and the flat-back Squat. It is through technique that a lifter expresses his strength.
Sequence of Movement The component parts of a technique consist of sequential movement elements which can be analysed separately for coaching purposes. When blended together in the correct order, there is what is known as a sequence of movement.

Where to Train

Undoubtedly the best place to train is where there is a qualified instructor or coach who has suitable training quarters, adequate equipment and changing facilities at his disposal. Examples are schools, clubs such as private weightlifting clubs, the Y.M.C.A., youth clubs, further education classes, various educational institutions, community sports centres and clubs organized by individual firms.

The guidance of the instructor is important in establishing correct habits from the start. Training in the company of experienced lifters can provide an excellent atmosphere, apart from learning by seeing others in action. A disciplined approach and knowledge may be acquired in a good club. Also, clubs usually participate in league lifting, which can be a useful introduction to competitive lifting.

Training at home in a basement or garage is not out of the question. Indeed many national champions have done much of their training at home. However, there can be drawbacks: for one thing, the necessary range of equipment and coaching are unlikely to be available. Some lifters combine club training sessions with supplementary training at home. The former are reserved for the more important work, while the latter complements the main training periods.

A First Weight-training Schedule

Persons embarking on their first weight-training schedule are keen to use too heavy a resistance to start with. It is important to ensure the application of safety precautions initially. This includes learning basic movements with light weights. The first fortnight is concerned with learning, using one set for each exercise. During that period safety procedures should be established. Then, gradual overloading in accordance with the Progressive Resistance Exercise (P.R.E.) principle is applied. During the second fortnight two sets may be used for each exercise. At the end of the second fortnight the weights should be such that the last repetition of each set can just be managed in good style. During the second month and thereafter three sets of each exercise may be practised.

Here is a simple schedule aimed at strengthening and developing the major muscle groups of the body.

		Sets and repetitions		
Exercise	*Reason/area developed*	*1st fortnight*	*2nd fortnight*	*2nd month*
1. Running, massive free exercises, and stretching exercises	Warm-up	—	—	—
2. Barbell curl	Biceps, brachialis, etc.	1 × 8–12	2 × 10	3 × 10
3. Press behind neck	Triceps, lateral and posterior deltoid and trapezius	1 × 8–12	2 × 10	3 × 10
4. Squat	Quadriceps and gluteals	1 × 8–16	2 × 12	3 × 12
5. Bench Press	Pectoralis major, anterior deltoid and triceps	1 × 8–12	2 × 10	3 × 10
6. Bentover rowing, medium grip	Latissimus dorsi and biceps	1 × 8–12	2 × 10	3 × 10
7. Heels raise	Gastrocnemius	1 × 12–20	2 × 15	3 × 20
8. Abdominal raise, with bent knees (no weights)	Rectus abdominis	1 × 8–16	2 × 12	2 × maximum reps

This schedule should be performed without long rest pauses between sets. Train three times weekly.

An Intermediate Weight-training Schedule

After at least three months of basic training, progression can be made on the lines as shown in the table on p. 46.

Starting to Train for Incentives or Competition

After the intermediate stage of general weight-training, early specialization follows, according to the aims of the weight-trainer. Some wish to specialize on strength and development, others think in terms of learning weightlifting skills. The latter group usually decides on some immediate objective such as attaining awards. Then competition, at a

Exercise	*Reason/area developed*	*Sets and repetitions*
1. Running and free exercise	Warm-up	—
2. Reverse curl	Forearms and biceps	3 × 10
3. Dumb-bells press	Deltoids, triceps and trapezius	3 × 10
4. Front Squat	*a.* strength	3 × 8
	b. fitness	2 × 15
5. Dumb-bells Bench Press	Pectoralis major, anterior deltoids and triceps	3 × 10
6. Bentover rowing, narrow grip	Latissimus dorsi and biceps	3 × 10
7. Power Clean	General, plus co-ordination	3 × 6
8. Heels raise	Gastrocnemius	3 × 20
9. Abdominal raise, with bent knees	Rectus abdominis	3 × 12

low level, follows. After that comes advanced training, aimed at increasingly higher standards of competition.

Having once decided to take up lifting of some kind, suitable beginners' schedules specifically for weightlifting or powerlifting have to be used. Examples of these are given in later chapters. Where highly skilled weightlifting movements are involved, much time has to be spent on the acquisition of skill with a light barbell. Various assistance exercises, especially those intended for the cultivation of balance and co-ordination, must be incorporated into the schedule. The services of a good coach or teacher are particularly valuable.

Five Weightlifting: Two Hands' Snatch

The Olympic Lifts

For competitive weightlifting purposes the I.W.F. recognizes two lifts which must be taken in sequence under the I.W.F. rules. These lifts are the Two Hands' Snatch, and the Two Hands' Clean and Jerk.

The I.W.F. recognizes World records on those lifts as well as the total for senior and junior lifters in the various bodyweight categories. Other records are recognized and registered by the appropriate federation or national governing body of weightlifting.

General Rules

1. The technique known as 'hooking' is permitted. It consists of covering the last joint of the thumb with the other fingers of the same hand at the moment of gripping.
2. In all lifts, pulling from the 'hang' is forbidden.
3. In all lifts, touching the bar against the legs below the knees shall not render the lift 'no lift'.
4. In all lifts, the referee must count as 'no lift' any unfinished attempt in which the bar has arrived at the height of the knees.
5. In all lifts, if the bar touches the thighs with a visible stop, it shall render the attempt 'no lift'. But, if during the pull the bar grazes or slides along the thighs without stopping, it shall not render the lift 'no lift'.
6. The use of grease, oil or liquid of any kind on the thighs to facilitate the sliding of the bar is forbidden.
7. In all lifts, touching the ground with any part of the body other than the feet shall render the attempt 'no lift'.
8. Any Clean in which the bar is placed on the chest before the turning over of the elbows shall render the attempt 'no lift'.
9. In any Clean, touching the thighs or knees with any part of the arm shall render the attempt 'no lift'.
10. In the Jerk, any apparent effort from the shoulders, if the lift is not completed, must be counted as 'no lift'. This includes lowering the body or bending the knees.
11. After the referee's signal to replace the bar, the lifter must lower the bar and not let it drop either deliberately or accidentally. The lifter must retain both hands on the barbell until it is replaced on the platform. If he releases his grip with one or both hands before

the barbell is replaced on the platform, this shall be considered dropping the bar, which shall render the attempt 'no lift'. There is no case for giving a lifter a warning the first time that he drops the barbell.

N.B. If a lifter is unable to straighten his arms, he must show this to the referees and jury before the contest.

Two Styles of Snatch

The first of the Olympic lifts is the Two Hands' Snatch. It is an athletic, explosive movement demanding strength, speed and skill. It is pleasing to watch—indeed it is regarded by many as an art form in motion. Even very big lifters move rapidly in this movement. A perfectly executed Snatch is most satisfying to the performer. A lifter can be extremely strong, but without efficient technique he cannot perform well on this lift. A strong pull must be augmented by neuromuscular co-ordination, balance, speed, timing and strong nerves.

Two styles are used: the 'squat' method and the 'split' or fore-and-aft method. In the first style the lifter pulls the weight upward and then dips under the barbell with a low squat. In the second style the lifter pulls the barbell upward, going under the bar with a lunge whereby one foot goes to the front and the other to the rear of the lifter. There are variations within each style.

International Rules for the Two Hands' Snatch

The I.W.F. rules state that the bar shall be placed horizontally in front of the lifter's legs. It shall be gripped, palms downward, and pulled in a single movement from the ground to the full extent of both arms vertically above the head, while either 'splitting' or bending legs. The bar shall pass with a continuous movement along the body of which no part other than the feet may touch the ground during the execution of the lift. The weight which has been lifted, must be maintained in the final motionless position, the arms and legs extended, the feet on the same line, until the referee's signal to replace the bar on the platform. The turning over of the wrists must not take place until the bar has passed the top of the lifter's head. The lifter may recover in his own time, either from a split or a squat.

The referee's signal shall be given as soon as the lifter becomes absolutely motionless in all parts of the body.

Incorrect Movements

1. Pulling from the hang.
2. Pause during the lifting of the bar.
3. Uneven extension of the arms.
4. Incomplete extension of the arms.

5. Finishing with a 'press-out'.
6. Bending and extending the arms during the recovery.
7. Touching the ground with the knee or buttocks or any part of the body other than the feet.
8. Leaving the platform during the execution of the lift.
9. Replacing the bar on the platform before the referee's signal.
10. Dropping the bar after the referee's signal to replace the bar.

Technique

Starting Position

a. Approach the bar in a brisk and businesslike manner. Squatters place their feet under the bar so that they are hip width or slightly less and with toes slightly outward. Splitters have their feet closer together, usually 15 cm (6 in) between the heels, with feet parallel or toes turned out. Certain national styles have the heels almost touching and toes turned well outward.

b. Grip the bar using a 'hook' grip if possible. The method of 'hooking' is to grip the bar with the fingers to the front and the Vs formed between the forefingers and thumbs pushed well into the top of the bar. The thumbs are bent so that their tips point towards the base of the little fingers, with the end part of the thumbs (distal phalanges) running parallel with the bar. The index and second fingers wrap firmly round both the thumbs and the bar. The third and fourth fingers are gripped around the bar.

   Those unable to use a hook grip should persevere with the technique. If impossible or very difficult to use, then grip the bar firmly with the fingers and the thumbs pressing firmly on to the top of the index fingers.

c. The hand spacing is determined by the following method. Stand with the arms raised horizontally then bend the elbows so that the forearms are at right angles to the upper arms. The distance measured between the index fingers is the standard hand spacing for the Snatch. In practice, however, this may be varied because of individual differences in technique, bone lengths and joint mobility. A narrower grip means the bar has to be lifted higher, but it enables considerable upward force to be exerted. By comparison, a wider grip means the bar need not be pulled quite so high. Moreover, a wide grip facilitates shoulder movement and makes the low 'recovery position' more stable due to greater control and a lower C of G of the bar.

d. The 'get set' or starting position is shown in Figure 2. The bar is directly over the bases of the big toes. The lifter usually looks directly forward with his head in natural alignment with his trunk, which is flat and inclined forward so that the gravity line of the shoulders is in front of the barbell. The arms are straight, with the elbows turned sideways. The shoulders are low and turned to the front. The hips are higher than the knees with an angle between the shin and thigh of approximately 90 degrees. The shins touch the bar. This is a strong, balanced starting position with the gravity lines of the bar and lifter over his feet, or base. (There is an alternative style used by a number of top lifters, whereby the lifter starts with hips lower than his knees and with a more upright trunk.)

Pull

Although there is only one pull, it is best considered in parts in order to give an analysis of what is really a very elaborate part of the Snatch.

a. Lift to the Knees The large muscles of the legs and hips initiate the pull off the platform to overcome the inertia of the bar. This part of the pull is fairly fast but slower than the second phase of the pull. Some lifters roll the bar along the platform into their shins before starting their pull. Referring to the diagrams in Figures 6*a* and 6*b*, it will be seen that when the bar reaches knee height the angle between the back and the platform remains the same. This is of the order of 16–25 degrees according to Webster (1967). At this stage, the arms are straight and the shoulders are forward. The shins are vertical. The lifter's C of G and that of the bar are over the lifter's feet. The upward path of the bar from the floor is slightly backward from the vertical. Splitters tend to have a straighter pull, while squatters tend to deviate rather more from the vertical.

b. Lift from the Knees As the bar passes the knees, the lifter is in his strongest pulling position. Simultaneously the hips and shoulders have been lifted upward. The hips now have to get under the bar, so they are moved forward and upward vigorously. This takes the bar slightly forward. The lifter's back has to extend, but the shoulders are kept forward, and the arms are kept straight with the elbows at the sides. As the bar passes the thighs many lifters ease the bar backward a little. The legs move to maximum extension but not completely straight so as to prevent the bar from going too far forward as well as avoiding difficulty later in getting the hips further forward. The lifter now rises on to the balls of his feet (sometimes on tiptoe) to obtain extra height of the bar which in theory should travel vertically upward. The top of the head is driven upward to assist. When on the balls of the feet, the area of the base is reduced but the gravity lines of the lifter and barbell coincide or are close together.

c. Conclusion of the Pull When the body is fully extended, the bar is in the region at the centre of, or just above, the front of the hips. Here the knees bend again, reflexly to preserve balance with the knees forward and in anticipation of moving the feet and legs. This is assisted by the elastic action of the hamstrings. Before the feet leave the platform the pull is finished by a shoulder shrug and a sideways bending of the arms.

The lifter must not overbalance at this point. The bar travels backward at the top of the pull mainly due to the angular motion of the whole system of the lifter and the bar. Some of the momentum of the lifter is transferred to the bar, which continues to travel upward even though the lifter himself can go no higher.

The velocity of the bar in the second phase of the pull is greater than in the initial stage.

Arm and Wrist Action

The elbows which have been raised sideways to keep them near the line of pull must not be yanked back indiscriminately. When the elbows can go no higher in the pull, the wrists keep the bar in motion at about mid-chest height. From a 'cocked' position, the wrists are flicked back rotating around the bar, spinning it about its own axis. Usually at this point the feet are moving into the squat or split.

When the feet contact the platform the arms are pressed straight as the split or squat finishes. The weight pushes the lifter down. The press-out to straight arms is fast, following continuously from the wrist action; it must be complete at the finish of the squat or split to avoid being judged a 'no lift'. The idea is to ensure that the arms are directly above the shoulder joints so as to preserve balance. The wrists must check any tendency of excess backward motion of the bar.

Receiving Positions

The low split or squat position is termed a 'receiving position'. *Speed into the receiving position is very important.* It cannot be achieved without a fast pull. Mobile shoulders, hips, knees and ankles are necessary for a low, balanced and controlled position. Those with long thighs in relation to shin lengths find it easier to get their hips nearer the platform—this helps stability.

a. Split Receiving Position The lifter moves his C of G forward to receive the weight. For better balance the lifter should aim to make both feet leave the platform simultaneously. The rear leg tends to leave the platform before the front leg—it has further to travel. As the feet leave the platform, the body lowers and the feet land in a split or fore-and-aft receiving position as shown in Figure 4. The weight is taken on a flat front foot and the ball of the rear foot, with the feet pointing straight forward or slightly turned inward. The rear foot typically lands first, pushing the body forward. The front foot lands immediately after the rear foot.

As the feet land in the split receiving position the hips continue their forward motion. The front knee is fully bent with the hips as close as possible to the heel. The rear knee is slightly flexed. The trunk is upright and the arms vertical, so that the gravity line of the weight passes through the shoulders and the hips. The head is upright, with the eyes looking forward.

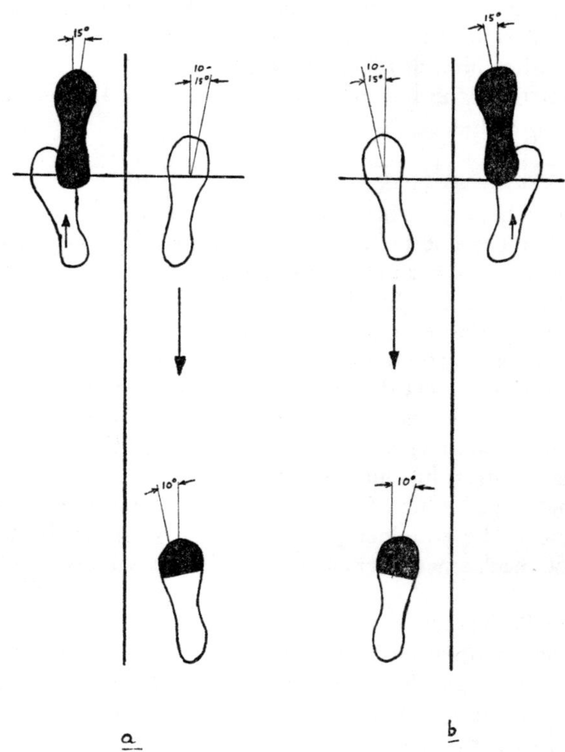

FIGURE 4. Position of the feet in the split snatch receiving position (Diagram *a* represents a lifter whose left foot moves foward in the split. Diagram *b* represents a lifter who leads with his right foot)

b. Squat Receiving Position There are a number of variations of the squat Snatch. The differences are seen in where the feet land, the foot spacing, the angle of the trunk and height of the hips in the receiving position. A sound, standard technique, capable of individual adjustment will be described.

The body drops rapidly after the bar has been pulled as high as possible. The feet move outward slightly to allow the hips to move forward close to the heels. A number of top Russian lifters squat snatch with their feet spaced out wider than their hips. The weight is taken evenly over both feet. The hips sink lower than the knees, which are moved outward a little. The knees point in the direction of the feet. The arm action is similar to that for the split Snatch.

The body is not vertical, but inclined slightly forward. There are many variations, but rarely is the angle formed between the back and the floor less than 50 degrees. Webster (1967) in his study of world-class lifters reports a range of 55½–80 degrees with an average back angle of 65 degrees. In most cases the head is kept erect with eyes looking forward, or at a point about 10 m (32 ft 6 in) away.

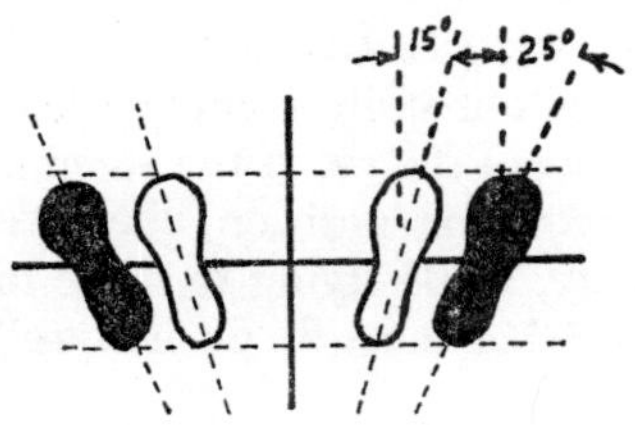

FIGURE 5. Position of the feet in the squat snatch receiving position

RECOVERY

a. Split Snatch Straighten both legs simultaneously. Then with the rear leg acting as a support and the trunk tilted slightly backward so that some of the weight is taken off the front foot, move the front foot back to the starting position. Then the rear foot is brought back to the starting position, so that it is in line. In the final, immobile position, the arms are kept vertically over the shoulder joints which are directly over the hips and feet.

b. Squat Snatch Lift the hips first, then the legs and hips straighten together. Usually the feet are brought closer together in readiness for the final, immobile position.

BREATHING

Many lifters inhale through the mouth prior to commencing the pull. Some breathe in as they pull. At the 'get set' position, breathing is augmented if a deep breath is taken; this is followed by a firm exhalation, which in turn is followed by a deep, deliberate inhalation for the lift. Exhalation occurs when the squat or split is made. Another breath is taken on rising.

LOWERING OF THE WEIGHT

The lifter must keep both hands on the barbell until it has reached knee height. In the case of a barbell loaded with discs with rubber protection, the hand control may be removed at waist height. The hands guide the weight down in front of the body; as they do so the elbows and knees bend so that the body lowers also.

In training, the competitive lowering procedure may damage the bar or platform. Usually two assistants, or training partners, take heavy weights from the overhead position. With light Snatches, the weights can be lowered under control in two phases in which there is a pause at the neck before the barbell is taken to the platform. In some gymnasia, there are rules forbidding the dropping of weights to the floor.

Procedure for Incomplete Lifts

Sometimes a lifter does not quite complete his lift. He then has to take evasive action to avoid injury. If the weight does not quite go to arm's length in the receiving position, the lifter pushes it forward from his head and body, while trying to move his hips backward. In the case of splitters, the bar must be pushed well clear of the leading leg.

In the situation where a lift goes to arm's length with backward travel, loss of control may be experienced whereby the lift simply cannot be saved. Here the procedure is to swing the arms backward in what has been termed a 'dislocation', to clear the head and body. The lifter has to move his body forward and let go of the barbell before it hits the platform.

Figure 6*a*. Sequence of movement of the split Snatch

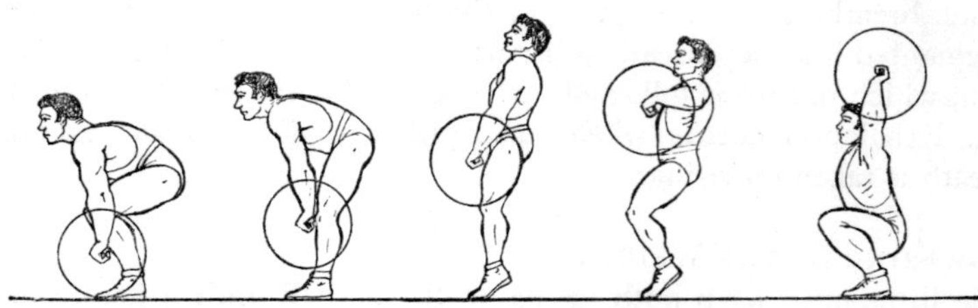

Figure 6*b*. Sequence of movement of the squat Snatch

Comments on the Snatch

As mentioned previously, there are variations in this lift. It is up to the coach to decide to what degree, and where, his lifter should depart from orthodox styles.

Beginners should be taught to pull straight. Other types of pull are rather sophisticated, involving S-shaped paths of the barbell. These are all right for certain athletic lifters with a high degree of perception of the various parts of their bodies. Coaches advocating other than vertical pulls should be aware of the subtle mechanics involved, as well as knowing the lifter's susceptibilities. The use of powdered resin on the hands helps the grip. Apply it to the front of the fingers and thumbs, the palm of the hand, and the ridge running along the side of the thumb and index fingers.

Boots with heels should be avoided if possible. However, some squatters find balance difficult without heels. There is no limit to the height.

Where support of the knees is considered necessary, the sizes of the support are restricted. The rules permit sleeve-type supports up to a maximum width of 25 cm ($9\frac{27}{32}$ in). Bandages must not exceed 8 cm ($3\frac{1}{8}$ in) in width. For the first five classes the length must not exceed 2·5 m (8 ft $1\frac{1}{2}$ in) and for the last five classes 3 m (9 ft 9 in). Bandages are best worn below the knee to give support to the ligaments at the sides of the knee and below the knee-cap. A combination of the elastic knee-cap and medical crepe bandages is forbidden. Wrist bandages may be worn, subject to a maximum width of 8 cm ($3\frac{1}{8}$ in), and length of 1·5 m (4 ft $10\frac{1}{2}$ in) and 2 m (6 ft 6 in) for the first five and last five classes, respectively.

A lifting belt may be worn. This is a useful aid for supporting not only the small of the back but the whole of the trunk. The belt is made of leather and its width must not exceed 10 cm ($3\frac{15}{16}$ in) at the widest part.

The problem of whether to squat or split has been debated many times. In general the squat appears to have slight advantages such as: pulling on both feet; it may be a little quicker; there is little tendency to lateral displacement; it is simpler; and so on. Therefore, if the young lifter has the ability to squat in balanced fashion controlling a barbell overhead, the squat Snatch should be taught. Otherwise, persevere with the split syle which can be equally effective when properly mastered. It really depends on the natural inclinations of the lifter and the views of the coach as to the style in which his lifter can achieve the best technique. Once again, it is a very individual problem.

Assistance Exercises

Assistance exercises fall into three categories. These are: technical assistance exercises containing elements of the Snatch and designed to help part of the snatching technique; strengthening exercises aimed at overcoming relative muscular weakness; and power exercises to increase strength and speed together. Some assistance exercises combine all of these features. In addition, there are flexibility exercises devised to help joint movement in relation to technique—these will be considered separately.

Do not perform more than two snatch assistance exercises if they are to be incorporated into a complete training schedule. The recommended sets and repetitions are only for general guidance and may be varied to suit individual needs.

Technical Assistance Exercises

a. Overhead Squats Squat with feet in the snatch receiving position and with the weight held overhead on straight arms, handspacing as for the Snatch. Splitters place their feet in the fore-and-aft receiving position, hands spaced as for the Snatch. Inhale on the descent, exhale on straightening the knees. Squat or lunge for 5 sets of 3–5 repetitions.

b. Snatch Balance Exercises

Splitters:

i. With legs almost straight, feet in the snatch receiving position and the barbell held with snatch grip on the collar bones, drive the bar slightly forward and upward with the arms. Dip the body downward and slightly forward into the low snatch receiving position.

ii. As for (i) above, but use a preliminary dip with a recoil jerk to start the bar moving. Then move into the snatch receiving position. More weight can be used in this exercise.

iii. This it a progression from (i) and (ii), incorporating a foot movement. The starting position is such that the rear foot is placed as for (i) but the front foot is placed about a foot-length behind its final position. The upward drive of the weight from the shoulders is initiated by a jerk and this is followed by a step with the front foot and at the same time lowering the body into the snatch receiving position as the bar is fixed overhead.

Breathe in as the weight is driven overhead and breathe out in the receiving position.

Squatters:

i. Stand with the bar held behind the neck with handspacing for the Snatch and resting across the shoulders. The feet are placed in the squat snatch receiving position. Press the weights overhead while dipping into the low receiving position.

ii. As for (i) above, but use a jerk start to get the weight moving. This enables more weight to be handled.

iii. This is a progression from (i) and (ii). Stand with feet in the snatch 'get set' position. Use a jerk action to move the bar upward and simultaneously move the feet outward to the squat snatch receiving position.

iv. In this movement, the barbell is held across the collar bone, using a snatch grip. Drive the weight overhead while dipping into the squat snatch receiving position. Use a press or jerk start, incorporating either fixed foot positions or a foot movement.

Breathe in as the weight is driven overhead and breathe out in the receiving position.

Perform 5 sets of 3–5 repetitions.

c. High Pulls This exercise is simply the pull of the Snatch performed separately. It incorporates identical elements of the snatch pulling technique. Take up the Snatch 'get set' position with the appropriate wide grip. Breathe in and pull the bar upward, keeping it close to the body. The sequence of the major muscle groups, taken in order, is: legs and hips; back; shoulder elevators; and arms. The top of the pull is around mid-chest height or above. Exhale on lowering. Perform 5 sets of 3–5 repetitions. This exercise can be performed with the assistance of wrist straps which wrap around the bar to give a better grip. They enable more weight to be used.

d. Snatch from Blocks Blocks of varying heights can be used to emphasize the later stages of the snatch pull, followed by movement into the receiving position and recovery. It is a modified training Snatch which can be used for improving timing or as a power builder. The starting height of the bar is adjusted by altering the height of the blocks. Use 5 sets of 5 repetitions for improving timing, or 5 sets of 3 repetitions for power training.

e. Hang Snatch This type of snatch exercise is performed with the bar 'hanging' down with the bar just off the floor. Perform 5 sets of 3 repetitions.

STRENGTH ASSISTANCE EXERCISES

a. Prone Hyperextension This important back exercise is shown in Plate 32. It can also be performed so that the front of the thighs lie across a bench, with a partner sitting across the back of the lifter's ankles to anchor them down. Padding, such as a piece of sponge rubber or a thick towel, placed on the bench in front of the thighs, makes the exercise comfortable. The aim is to arch the lower back as much as possible, holding the terminal position for about a second. Inhale as the effort is made; exhale when resuming the starting position. Perform 3–5 sets of 10 repetitions with moderate poundages.

b. 'Good Morning' Exercise This is another back-strengthening exercise. The lifter places the barbell across his shoulders. He stands with his feet hip-width apart. The shins are vertical and knees slightly bent. With a flat back and head lifted, the lifter bends at the waist until his back reaches a position 10–15 degrees from the horizontal. The hips are outside the feet as in Plate 32. The back is then rotated to the upright starting position. Inhale as the effort is made; exhale on lowering. Perform 3 sets of 10 repetitions.

c. Bentover Rowing This bodybuilding movement has been used successfully by Olympic weightlifters. Stand with feet hip width apart, legs slightly bent and back flat in the horizontal plane. With a snatch-width grip pull the bar towards the chest. Hold for a fraction of a second and lower. Inhale as the arms bend; exhale on lowering the weight. Perform 5 sets of 5 repetitions.

d. Upright Rowing with Shoulder-width Grip Pick up the barbell with hands shoulder-width apart. Keep the body straight, then bend the elbows, keeping them high while pulling the bar upward to shoulder height. Breathe in on the upward pull. Use occasionally for variety, performing 5 sets of 5 repetitions.

The following are the chief exercises for increasing the strength of the thumbs, fingers and hands. Repetitions and sets are usually low: the aim is to make the forearms, fingers, thumbs and hands work hard. They will tire when exercised sufficiently.

e. Pinch Grip Use heavy, smooth, disc weights. Simply grip these between the fingers and thumb, then lift the disc from the floor. Hold for about a second, then lower or grip with the other hand. Alternate the hands. Breathe freely.

f. Dumb-bell Gripping Using a dumb-bell with a thick handle about 5 cm (2 in) diameter, transfer the bell from hand to hand. Breathe freely.

g. Chinning the Beam Use a thumbs and fingers grip only to chin the beam. Hang by straight arms from the beam, then bend the elbows until the chin touches the beam. Inhale on the effort; exhale when lowering.

h. Wrist Roller Exercise This exercise works the forearm and all the gripping muscles. Whilst breathing freely wind the weight up with the roller with alternate movements of the hands, operating with as great a range of movement as possible. Control the lowering for extra effects.

Power Assistance Exercises

a. Power Snatch Assume the snatch 'get set' position. Keeping the barbell close to the legs, then close to the body, pull it to arm's length overhead without moving the feet and with only a slight knee dip to make the movement smooth and quick. Breathe in just before the

initial pull. The power Snatch can be performed from blocks: the higher the blocks, the greater the emphasis on the upper part of the pull. Perform 5 sets of 2–5 repetitions, according to weight used.
b. High Dead Lifts with Snatch Grip Adopt the snatch 'get set' position. Pull the bar to waist height, rising on the toes and thrusting the hips forward and upward as the bar passes the hips. Try to finish with a shoulder shrug. Inhale just before the pull. Since very heavy weights are used perform 3 or 4 sets of 2–3 repetitions only.
c. Snatch from Belt Using a snatch grip, the barbell is laid across the lifter's belt. Starting with a little dip, followed by a full extension of the body, shoulder shrug and arm pull snatch the weight. Emphasize timing and speed. Inhale prior to the dip. Perform 3–5 sets of 3 repetitions.
d. Shoulder Shrug Using a snatch grip, stand upright with the bar resting across the thighs. Elevate the shoulders as high as possible without bending the elbows. Inhale during the shrug; exhale as the shoulders are lowered. Perform 5 sets of 5 repetitions.
e. Power Clean with Snatch Grip Adopt the snatch 'get set' position. With snatch pulling technique, elevate the bar to the shoulders. Then, without foot movement and only a little knee dip, receive the bar across the collar bone and the front of the shoulders. The wrists turn over powerfully, with elbows under the bar. Inhale just before the pull. Perform 5 sets of 2–3 repetitions.

Flexibility Exercises

Flexible hips, ankles and shoulders are necessary for efficient snatching. Squat snatchers, in particular, have to pay attention to mobility in these joints. Where a joint is tight it will hamper efficiency. For a tight joint to become more mobile it has to be stretched against the joint's protective reflex at the end of the joint's range of movement. The antagonist muscle has to be lengthened. 'Free' exercise, light resistance movement or partner exercises are used for 2–3 sets of 10–15 repetitions. Breathe freely. The following exercises are used by weightlifters.

a. Shoulder Mobilizing Exercises

i. Arms circling slowly backward. Make the upper arms brush past the ears while keeping the arms straight.
ii. Kneel on the floor with arms parallel and stretched out so that the palms of the hands are flat on the floor as in Plate 34. Push the head, chest and shoulders towards the floor with a rebound.
iii. Take a wide grip on an exercise bar which rests across the front of the thighs. Keeping the arms straight, raise them forward and upward, then overhead so that the bar can be lowered behind the head. Reverse the procedure. The difficulty can be increased by

pulling outward along the bar and using a narrower grip. This exercise is used by squat snatchers.

b. Hip Mobilizing Exercises

i. Stand on one leg while grasping with one hand wallbars or a partner. Keeping the other leg straight, lift it forward and upward as high as it will go; then lower it to the floor and extend it backward and upward as high as possible. Repeat with the other leg.

ii. Starting position as for (i); raise the leg sideways as high as possible. Repeat with the other leg.

iii. Squat on one leg with the other leg straight and the foot raised up on a couple of disc weights or a bench. Straighten the bent knee a little then squat low so that the thigh is stretched. Repeat on the other leg.

iv. Sit on the floor with legs straight and apart. Bend forward as far as possible with arms outstretched. Press downward to stretch the back of the thighs.

v. Squat snatchers can improve their receiving position by practising this exercise. Squat as low as possible in the receiving position. Push the knees outward against the resistance of a partner, trying to push the hips forward. Relax, then repeat with strong pressure.

c. Ankles

i. Lunges, with and without weights help. Try to push the knee as far forward as possible. Repeat with the other knee.

ii. Squatters practise low squats without weights trying to push the knees outward and downward, thereby reducing the angle formed between the floor and the shins.

d. Hook Grip Exercise

Provided the lifter's hands and fingers are not too small, the hook grip can be improved counteracting any stiffness of the joints of the thumb. Push the tip of the thumb across the palm of the hand towards the base of the little finger, hold it there or near to it for about three seconds. Repeat, trying to stretch a little further. Alternate the hands.

Training Methods

The snatch is a complex lift, demanding special training. In the early stages time has to be spent in repetitive practice with light weights in order to master the correct pattern of the motor skill involved and to develop speed of movement. As training becomes advanced (see Chapter 7), the lifter is concerned less with learning and more with peak form in competition.

A Beginner's Schedule

The following is based on a top Snatch 70 kg (154¼ lb). The schedule is devised to improve technique and strength of a relatively inexperienced lifter who has established an adequate foundation and is ready to progress further.

Warm-up: running, jumping, free exercises and stretching movements, 5 minutes
Snatch with bar only: 2 × 8
Snatch: 3 × 5—40 kg (88 lb)
Snatch balance exercise: 3 × 5
Snatch: 2 × 5—45 kg (99 lb); 2 × 4—50 kg (110 lb)
3 × 3—55 kg (121¼ lb); 2 × 2—57·5 kg (126¼ lb)

This schedule may be incorporated into the overall training programme. An additional assistance exercise plus flexibility exercises may be performed at the end of the full schedule. If possible, the weight should be increased by 2·5 kg (5½ lb) every three weeks. Aim for good style and do not force increases. Train three times weekly with workouts lasting from one and half to two hours.

Progression

As an early beginner the lifter will have practised the Snatch with an intensity of about 50 per cent of his bodyweight. As he becomes more experienced his workouts change from a schedule of a few exercises performed at a low barbell intensity to a schedule of more exercises of greater intensity and a higher volume of training load. As his physical and technical capabilities develop he will graduate from an early beginner's status to a different category.

Six Weightlifting: Two Hands' Clean and Jerk

The second of the Olympic lifts is the Two Hands' Clean and Jerk. As its name suggests, it is a two-part movement, and it demands great strength, athletic qualities sound technique and concentration. It is an unparalleled test and challenge for any strength athlete since it is composed of two consecutive all-out movements necessitating an unusual form of staying power. Very often it is the deciding factor in who wins or places in the competition.

Many athletes in heavy field events use the Clean and Jerk as an important all-round, co-ordinated power movement. Several budding hammer-throwers and shot-putters have benefited from incorporating this lift into their training.

The top lifters in the world approach a performance of two and three-quarter times their own bodyweight in this lift. Flyweights exceed 140 kg (308½ lb), while superheavies have jerked over 242·5 kg (534½ lb).

The Clean consists of a two-handed pull to the waist followed by a low split or squat receiving position as the bar is taken into the neck. The Jerk is invariably executed with a split.

International Rules for the Two Hands' Clean and Jerk
The I.W.F. rules state:

CLEAN
The bar shall be placed horizontally in front of the lifter's legs. It shall be gripped, palms downward, and brought in a single movement from the ground to the shoulders, while either 'splitting' or bending the legs. The bar must not touch the chest before the final position. It shall then rest on the clavicles or on the chest or on the arms fully bent. The feet shall be returned to the same line, legs straight, before performing the Jerk. The lifter may make this recovery in his own time.

JERK
Bend the legs and extend them as well as the arms so as to bring the bar to the full stretch of the arms vertically extended. Return the feet to the same line, arms and legs extended and await the referee's signal to replace the bar on the platform.

The referee's signal shall be given as soon as the lifter becomes absolutely motionless in all parts of the body.

1. Assorted weight-training equipment

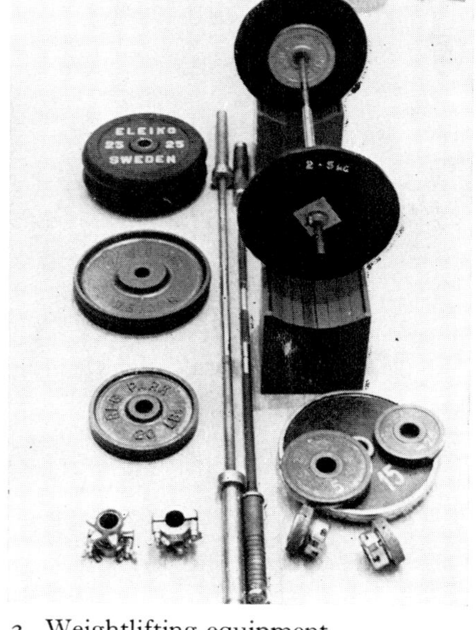

2. Weightlifting equipment

3. The Bulgarian electrodinamograph

4. Squat stands and Kolev (Bulgaria) push jerking
(Kolev won the World middleweight title in 1974 and was voted Bulgaria's most popular athlete)

5. Reverse curl—starting position
6. (*above right*) Reverse curl—finishing position
7. (*right*) Upright rowing—starting position

Exercises performed by Canadian middleweight, Larry Yessie

8. (*left*) Upright rowing—finishing position
9. (*below left*) Press behind neck—starting position
10. (*below right*) Press behind neck—finishing position

11. The 'get set' position of Stan Stanzyck (U.S.A.), former World 82·5 kg champion
(Note the flat back, straight arms and forward shoulder position)
(*G. Kirkley photo*)

12. Kailajarvi (Finland) demonstrating the snatch pull

13. Pervushin (U.S.S.R.), 1973 World 110 kg champion, during the snatch pull
(Note the flat back, straight arms and shoulder position)

14. Rigert (U.S.S.R.), former World 90 kg champion, in the squat snatch receiving position
(*O. State photo*)

15. George Newton (Great Britain), 1974 Commonwealth 67·5 kg champion, snatching 110 kg ($242\frac{1}{2}$ lb)

16. Palinski (Poland), 90 kg lifter, cleaning a World record weight of 177·5 kg ($396\frac{3}{4}$ lb)
(This is a perfect split Clean)

17. Baszanowski (Poland) pulling in the Clean
(Note the straight arms. Was Poland's greatest 67·5 kg lifter, setting twenty-seven World and sixty-one National records)

18. Heuser (G.D.R.), 110 kg plus lifter, in an excellent position in the clean pull
(Note the flat back and the straight arms)

19. Rigert (U.S.S.R.), 90 kg lifter, showing perfect balance in the squat Clean
(The weight is well into the neck, the elbows are high and the knees turned out)

20. Shopov (Bulgaria), 90 kg lifter, jerking 192·5 kg (424$\frac{1}{4}$ lb) at the 1972 Olympic Games in Munich where he gained a silver medal

21. Split snatch balance exercise—start

22. Split snatch balance exercise—finish

23. Squat snatch balance exercise—behind neck start

24. Squat snatch balance exercise—in front of neck start

25. Squat snatch balance exercise—finish

26. Split lunges—start

27. Split lunges—finish

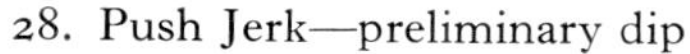
28. Push Jerk—preliminary dip

29. Push Jerk—finish

30. Half Squat

31. 'Good morning' exercise—start

32. Prone hyperextension—finish

33. Thigh-suppling exercise

34. Shoulder-mobilizing exercise

35. Squat—taking the bar from the stands

36. Start of the Squat

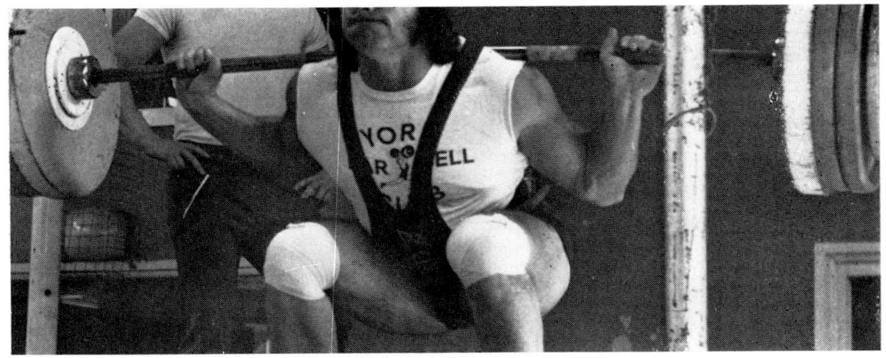

37. (*middle*) Squat with tops of thighs below the horizontal

38 (*below*) Loaders handing the barbell to the lifter in readiness for the Bench Press
(The lifter is Joe Whitlam, former British 90 kg record-holder)

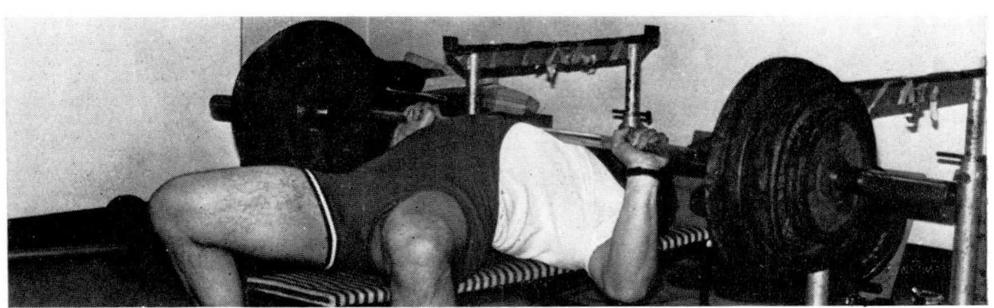

39. (*top*) Bench Press—bar held at the chest just before upward drive
40. (*middle*) Bench Press—during upward drive of arms
41. (*bottom*) Finish of the Bench Press with loaders standing by to take the barbell
42. (*left*) Start of the Dead Lift
(Note the reversed grip)

43. (*top*) Finish of the Dead Lift
(Note the straight legs and trunk demonstrated by Ron Collins, Britain's greatest powerlifter)
44. (*above*) John Peglar, 90 kg powerlifter, concentrating during a heavy Dead Lift

facing page

45. (*top*) Gerald Mills, British paraplegic heavyweight champion, demonstrating the starting position of the paraplegic Bench Press
(Note the use of leg straps which are permitted when the lifter has spasm of one or both legs)
46. (*second*) Barbell pressed to arm's length in the paraplegic Bench Press
(The lifter is Ralph Rowe, 1974 Commonwealth champion in the 85 kg class)
47. (*third*) Stuart Lindley, British featherweight champion, demonstrating the starting position of the Lateral Raise, Lying
48. (*fourth*) Finish of the Lateral Raise, Lying
49. (*bottom*) Start of the pull over part of the Pull Over and Press on Back

50. Start of the press of the Pull Over and Press on Back

51. Finish of the press of the Pull Over and Press on Back

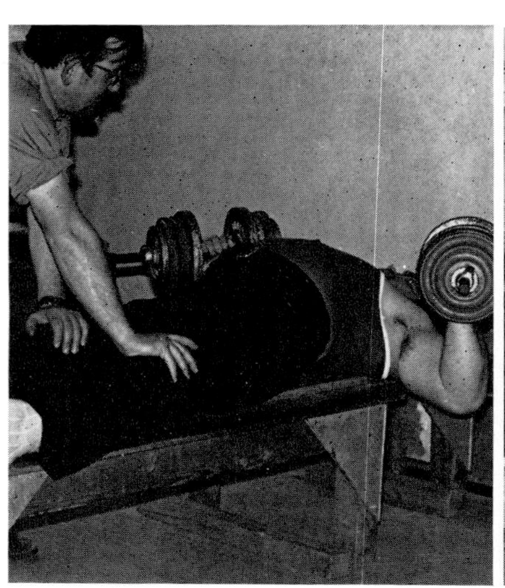

52. Ron Nicholls, British paraplegic team coach, steadying the knees of paraplegic Gerald Mills, at the start of the dumb-bells Press on Back

53. Finish of the dumb-bells Press on Back

IMPORTANT REMARK: After the Clean and before the Jerk, the lifter may assure the position of the bar. This must not lead to confusion. It cannot mean in any case, granting a second movement to the lifter, but of allowing him

a. either to withdraw his thumbs or to 'unhook' if he has used this method; or
b. if the bar is placed too high and impedes his breathing or causes a pain, to lower it in order to rest it on his shoulders; or
c. to change the width of his grip.

Incorrect Movements

Clean

1. Any unfinished attempt at pulling in when the bar has reached at least the height of the knees.
2. Pulling from the 'hang'.
3. Cleaning in two or more movements.
4. Touching the ground with the knee or buttocks or any part of the body other than the feet.
5. Any Clean in which the bar touches a part of the trunk before the final position at the shoulders.
6. Cleaning in the squat position, touching the knees or thighs with any part of the arms.
7. Leaving the platform during the execution of the lift.

Jerk

8. Any apparent effort of jerking which is not completed.
9. Uneven extension of the arms.
10. Pause during the extension of the arms.
11. Bending and extending the arms during the recovery.
12. Leaving the platform during the execution of the lift.
13. Replacing the bar on the platform before the referee's signal.
14. Dropping the bar after the referee's signal to replace the bar.

Technique of the Clean

Starting Position

a. A businesslike approach without fuss or delay is recommended. Walk up to the bar and assume the 'get set' position. The hands are spaced a little wider than shoulder width, measured between the index fingers. Grasp the bar firmly using the 'hook' grip.
b. As with the Snatch the barbell's axis lies over the base of each of the big toes.
c. The heels are usually placed hip width apart or a little less.

feet are parallel or are turned outward slightly. Although some Far Eastern lifters use a much narrower foot spacing with the feet well turned out, this is not generally recommended.

d. The back is kept flat and inclined forward with the head in natural alignment with the spine. The eyes look forward and down, focusing a few metres ahead.

e. The hips are higher than the knees. The angle between the thighs and shins averages a little more than a right angle, but is dependent on the length of the bony levers of the lifter.

f. The arms are straight and internally rotated so that the elbows turn outward. The gravity line of the shoulders is forward of the barbell.

g. The shoulders are kept low, but higher than the hips. (There is an alternative style used by a number of top lifters, whereby the lifter starts with hips lower than his knees and with a more upright trunk.)

PULL

a. The initial lift from the platform is effected by a combined leg and hip drive, during which the arms are kept straight and the angle of the back kept virtually constant. This part of the pull is fairly fast but slower than the second phase. A powerful pull in the first phase helps the second phase.

b. The aim is for the bar to travel vertically upward; however, its pathway will deviate somewhat from this ideal straight path. The first deviation occurs just after the bar leaves the platform, when the bar is eased back to the shins to bring it over the middle of the lifter's feet.

c. When the bar is at knee height, the shins are vertical, the arms are straight and the shoulders are kept forward of the bar.

d. The movement then speeds up with the back moving to a more upright position. As the bar brushes the thighs, the hips are thrust forward and upward, while retaining straight arms. This carries the bar slightly forward.

e. As the bar passes the hips, the lifter rises on to the balls of his feet. The rest of his body fully extends, followed by a shoulder shrug. After this the arms start to bend. The velocity of the bar in the second phase of the pull is greater than in the initial stage.

ARM AND WRIST ACTION

a. When the barbell has reached approximately waist height both feet are moved simultaneously in the direction of the clean receiving position.

b. At the same time the barbell is rotated about its own axis by a powerful wrist action backward which takes the bar from the front of the waist to the front of the neck, resting on the collar bone.

c. The elbows move rapidly from a point above the bar to a position in front of and below the bar. The elbows are thrust forward and high so that the bar is balanced securely behind the shoulders.

d. During the arm and wrist action the bar travels slightly backward in a loop-like pathway. The hook grip is maintained throughout. The action of both arms must be symmetrical and the bar must be kept level.

Receiving Positions

As the arms and feet move after full extension of the lifter, the bar tends to continue its upward motion. Before it starts to descend under the pull of gravity the lifter has to get underneath the bar very quickly in a deep receiving position which may be a split or a squat. A fast-moving lifter moves his feet before the bar lowers; at the same time he exerts upward pressure on the bar.

a. Split Clean Receiving Position In this version of the clean receiving position, there is a tendency for the rear foot to contact the platform first. Reaction causes the body to move slightly forward. The rear foot travels directly backward behind its corresponding hip joint. The front foot moves directly in front of its corresponding hip joint. The lifter has to position his hips quickly under the bar for balance. The hips move below the level of the front knee, just forward of the shoulders. The front shin is inclined forward so that the front knee is ahead of the foot. The gravity line of the head and shoulders passes through the hip joint. The front foot is flat on the platform and pointing directly ahead. Only the toes and the ball of the rear foot make contact with the platform, while the shin of the rear leg lies approximately parallel with the platform. Since the lifter has to contend with the downward momentum of his own body and the bar, care has to be taken not to touch the platform with the rear knee.

b. Squat Clean Receiving Position It is recommended that both feet simply move simultaneously sideways to land in a deep squat with toes turned outward for balance. Some lifters move slightly forward in this manoeuvre; others move backward. The aim is to be in balance. The elbows are kept high and must not touch the thighs or knees. The gravity line of the head and shoulders passes through the hip joint. The shins are inclined forward and the calves and thighs are in contact. Pressure must be exerted by the whole of the soles of the feet. If the lifter has moved forward, he must consciously press harder into the platform with his toes; conversely, if he moves backward, firm pressure at the heels is important. However, excess forward or backward travel usually results in a failure to clean effectively.

RECOVERY

a. The splitter tilts the bar backward a little while straightening both legs. Then using the rear leg as a buttress, the weight is lessened over the front foot, which is then moved back to a position directly below the lifter's hips. The bar is then tilted forward a little, followed by a movement of the rear foot which is brought in line with the front foot. The lifter has now recovered to the upright position in readiness for the Jerk.

b. The squatter recovers from the low squat Clean by keeping the elbows high to prevent the bar falling off the collar bone. He raises his hips first, then simultaneously straightens his legs and hips. The knees point in the same direction as the feet. The hips are pushed forward until they are in the same vertical line as the lifter's shoulders and ankles. When in the upright position, the lifter prepares for the Jerk.

Technique of the Jerk

a. The lifter usually unhooks his thumbs and places them firmly on the outside of the fingers. If the bar is too high, or the breathing is impaired, or the lifter finds it painful, the bar may be lowered to the shoulders. Another readjustment permitted within the rules is a change of the width of the lifter's grip.

b. After any adjustments have been made, the elbows are moved so that they are 45 degrees from the vertical. The body is upright and the weight evenly distributed over the soles of the feet. The lifter dips with a knee bend as far as the flexibility of the ankle joints will permit. On average this dip is about 15 cm (6 in). The trunk is kept vertical and the feet remain flat on the platform.

c. At this juncture, the legs are straightened vigorously, while the arms drive the bar upward in a synchronized manner. By the time the bar arrives just in front of the chin, the lifter has risen on to his toes in readiness for the feet to move into a split receiving position. The arms continue to drive upward and fractionally backward to achieve a solid elbow lock with the arms vertically over the shoulders.

d. The split for the Jerk is not as deep as that of the Clean. There is a slight bending of the front knee with the hips usually a little higher than the front knee. The rear leg is straight, while the front shin is vertical. The barbell's gravity line passes through the lifter's shoulder and hip joints.

e. To recover to the upright position the front foot is brought under the hips, then the rear foot is drawn alongside the front foot. The knees, hips and elbows are firmly braced to provide a final immobile position, which will be indicated by the referee's signal to lower the barbell.

f. To lower the bar the lifter keeps both hands on the bar while bending his arms, hips and knees. He must try to keep the bar horizontal and should not let go of the bar until it is at knee height. (If rubber-protected disc weights have been loaded on to the barbell, it is permissible to release the barbell at waist height.)

BREATHING

a. Inhale through the mouth just before the pull for the Clean. Exhale on recovery.
b. Just prior to the Jerk, take a deep breath through the mouth, exhaling as the weight is jerked.
c. Inhale again on the recovery from the Jerk. Hold the breath in the final, controlled position. Exhale during the lowering of the weight.

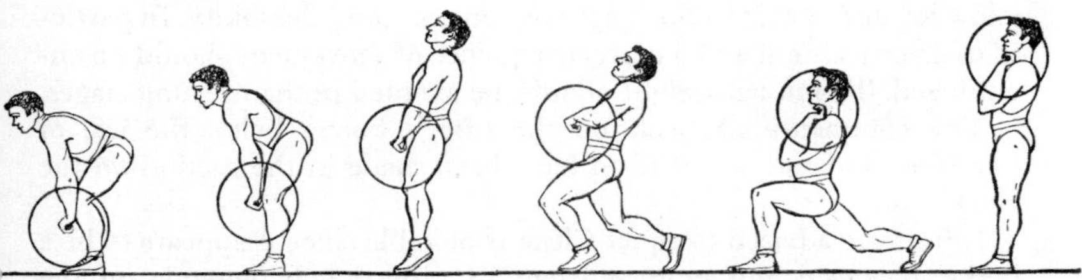

FIGURE 7*a*. Sequence of movement of the split Clean

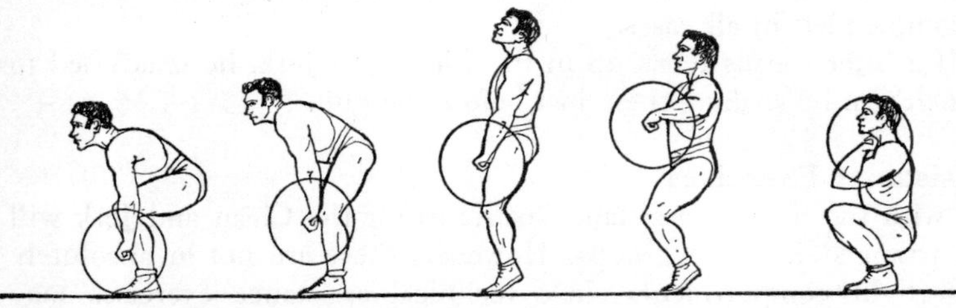

FIGURE 7*b*. Sequence of movement of the squat Clean

FIGURE 7*c*. Sequence of movement of the Jerk

PROCEDURE FOR INCOMPLETE LIFTS

In the case of a Clean that is missed, the weight must be pushed forward and away from the lifter. In the case of a splitter, care must be taken to push the barbell well clear of the front thigh and knee.

When a Jerk fails, the lifter must push the weight forward and away from his body, sometimes stepping back concurrently. Occasionally a Jerk is lost backward and overhead. Here the lifter guides the weight with his hands so that it continues its journey to the rear; at the same time he steps quickly forward.

Comments on the Clean and Jerk

As with the Snatch, there are variations in the Clean and Jerk. However, coaches are advised to keep novices and lifters of intermediate standard on the basic styles described. Small variations may be made to allow for differences in the length of bones or joint flexibility. In particular, a vertical pull and a correct sequence of movement should be encouraged. Too much weight should be avoided in the learning stages.

The comments on heels on the lifter's boots, belts, the use of bandages and the use of resin have been made in the section on the Snatch lift.

Lifters are advised to squat Clean if possible since it appears to be a better balanced and more efficient lift, but much depends on the individual in question. The tendency to Jerk without foot movement as seen in certain lifters is not advocated. Jerking with a split is recommended in all cases.

If a lifter's arms tense up in the Clean and Jerk, he is advised to relax them by shaking them just before the pull.

Assistance Exercises

As with the Snatch, assistance exercises for the Clean and Jerk will be arranged in three groups. However, these are not in absolutely watertight compartments since technical assistance exercises may contain power or strengthening aspects as well.

Beginners should not perform more than two of these in their workouts if they are in addition to training on other lifts. Concentrate on deficient areas first, working on them for at least six to eight weeks. The recommended sets and repetitions may be varied to suit individual needs.

TECHNICAL ASSISTANCE EXERCISES

a. Split Lunges Place the feet in the split clean receiving position. Keeping the bar close to the throat with elbows high, lower the body from a straight-legged position into the deep split clean receiving position. Then straighten the legs and repeat. Inhale on lowering and

exhale on straightening the legs. Perform 5–8 sets of 3–5 repetitions.
b. Front Squats Place the feet in the squat clean receiving position. Keep the bar close to the throat with elbows high. From the standing position lower the body to the deep squat clean receiving position. Straighten the hips first and then use both legs and hips together until the lifter is upright. Breathing, sets and repetitions as for (*a*) above.
c. Jerk Balance Exercises

i. Hold a barbell behind the shoulders using a jerk grip and place feet in the jerk fore-and-aft receiving position. From a straight-legged position simultaneously press the weight overhead while bending the knees into the split jerk receiving position. Inhale as the weight is driven overhead and exhale as it is lowered for the next repetition. Perform 5 sets of 3–5 repetitions.
ii. Perform the exercise as for (i) but use a preliminary jerk before dipping into the receiving position. More weight can be used than for (i). Breathing, sets and repetitions as for (i).
iii. Using a relatively light weight, stand in a position as if about to jerk. Then, without a preliminary dip, quickly move the feet and drop into the jerk receiving position. Inhale just before moving and exhale as the feet split. Perform 5 sets of 3 repetitions.

d. High Pulls with Clean Grip This exercise is the pull for the Clean performed separately. Take up the clean 'get set' position, breathe in and pull the bar to waist height, delaying any bending of the arms for as long as possible. The correct sequence of the major muscle groups, taken in order is: legs and hips; back; shoulder elevators; and arms. This exercise can be performed with the help of wrist straps, if very heavy weights are to be used. Perform 5–8 sets of 3–5 repetitions.
e. Clean Grip Pulls from Blocks Arrange the blocks so that the clean pull is accentuated at the desired height. Then complete the pull from that height, finishing with a shoulder shrug. Inhale on the pull, exhale on lowering. Use 5 sets of 5 repetitions for improving technical aspects of the pull. Use 5–8 sets of 2–3 repetitions for power training.
f. Cleans from Blocks Perform this movement as for exercise (*e*), only complete the Clean by going into a low split or squat clean receiving position.

STRENGTH ASSISTANCE EXERCISES

The first three exercises have been described in the previous chapter.
a. Prone Hyperextension
b. 'Good Morning' Exercise
c. Gripping Exercises
d. Halting Dead Lift From the clean 'get set' position, a heavy barbell is lifted to the knees where it is held for 2–5 seconds according to the effect it is desired to achieve. It is important to assume the exact

position of the 'lift to the knees' in the clean pull. From this isometric position the lifter completes the clean pull as fast as possible. This movement is a favourite advanced training exercise advocated by B.A.W.L.A. National Technical Adviser and former National Coach, Al Murray, who used it in the preparation of former World Middle-heavy champion, Louis Martin, O.B.E. Perform 2 repetitions with a poundage equal to the lifter's best Clean, plus 10 per cent; then perform another 1 or 2 repetitions with a poundage equivalent to the best Clean, plus 20 per cent.

e. Straight-legged Dead Lift This exercise is described in Chapter 11. For assisting the Clean start light for a few weeks, then build up to a maximum weight of the lifter's best Clean plus 20 per cent. Use 5 sets of 3–4 repetitions.

f. Overhead Supports Use overhead training racks or the assistance of two training partners to place a heavy weight overhead in the jerk receiving position with locked arms. Unlock the elbows a little, then lock them again for a second or two. Inhale on locking and exhale on unlocking. Repeat for 5 sets of 2 repetitions.

g. Abdominal Raise on Inclined Bench This exercise is to strengthen the muscles at the front of the trunk—an area which is under pressure in the Clean and often neglected by many lifters. Fix the ankles under the retaining strap at the top of the inclined board or bench. Hold a light barbell in front of the neck and sit up. Inhale as the effort is made; exhale on lowering. Perform 3 sets of 10 repetitions.

POWER ASSISTANCE EXERCISES

a. Squat See Chapter 9 for training details of the Deep Knees' Bend, or Squat. Also, see details of the half and quarter Squat.

b. Jump Squat This exercise is for improving a lifter's explosive power. Place a relatively light barbell behind the neck and stand as if about to perform an orthodox squat. With a controlled movement, lower into a squat position, recovering by jumping vigorously upward and as high as possible, aiming to drive the body well into the air. Land on the floor with a dip of the knees, then gently lower to a squat position. Jump upward again and repeat. Inhale on the descent and exhale forcefully on jumping upward. Perform 3 sets of 10 repetitions.

c. Vertical Jump with Dumb-bells This exercise will improve a lifter's abdominal strength and explosive power of the legs. Stand with the feet in the squat position while holding a pair of light dumb-bells in the hands. Squat down, then jump vigorously upward, taking the dumb-bells to the shoulders and knees to the chest. Inhale on lowering, exhale forcefully on jumping upward. Repeat for 3 sets of 10 repetitions.

d. Shoulder Shrugs These are described in Chapter 5. For assistance in the Clean, use handspacing as for the Clean.

e. Power Clean This is a basic explosive power builder, which is a favourite among many top lifters. It is really a Clean without foot movement, using only a small dip. Perform as for a squat Clean but pull the bar higher than usual, making a shallow squat for the receiving position. Use a pyramid progression of increasing poundage with decreasing repetitions (5, 4, 3, 2, 1) or 5 sets of 2–3 repetitions.

f. Clean from Belt This exercise is particularly good for improving the arm action and general body and leg movement in the transition from the top of the pull to the receiving position. The lifter stands with the barbell resting on his belt. He has his knees slightly forward, body approximately vertical, with elbows slightly bent and turned to the sides. He dips slightly and then recoils upward while moving on to his toes. Then follows a shoulder shrug which in turn is followed by a foot movement and rotation of the bar. The lifter then moves rapidly into either the split or squat clean receiving position. He then recovers to the upright position in the same way as he would following a normal Clean. Inhale just before dipping; exhale forcefully when dropping under the bar. Inhale again in the receiving position. Perform 5–6 sets of 2 repetitions.

g. Push Jerk This is a jerk exercise without foot movement. It is one of the most important jerk assistance exercises. Stand with a barbell at the shoulders as if about to jerk. Dip in the usual way, recoiling upward with leg and hip power. At the same time drive vigorously upward with the arms. Without moving the feet, continue pushing the barbell to arm's length. Inhale just before dipping; exhale as the barbell moves overhead. Perform 5–8 sets of 2–3 repetitions.

h. Jerk Behind Neck This exercise is particularly good for correcting any tendency to jerk forward. It is a tremendous power booster and was used by the author prior to breaking the British lightheavyweight record on the Clean and Jerk lift. Using a jerk grip, the lifter starts with the barbell held behind his neck and resting above his shoulders. Assistants can lift the bar to this position, or it can be taken off squat stands. The elbows are kept in a slightly forward position. After a preliminary dip, during which the chest is kept vertical, the lifter then uses leg, hip and arm power to drive the bar vertically to arm's length. As the bar reaches a point half way up the back of the head he moves his legs and feet rapidly into the split receiving position. Inhale on the dip; exhale as the bar is driven upward. Perform 5 sets of 2 repetitions.

i. Pressing Movements If a lifter's Jerk is sound technically, but lacks fundamental power especially in the triceps and deltoid muscles, a short course of presses may be advocated. Training presses are essentially arm and shoulder exercises performed without leg or body movement. They should not be confused with the now obsolete Olympic press. The lifter stands, sits, or lies on a bench with a barbell or dumb-bells held at the shoulders and simply straightens his arms. He inhales on the effort and exhales as the weight is returned to the starting position.

Choose one or two of the following presses for inclusion twice or three times a week into the main training programme. Novices are advised to use training presses to build a strong foundation for jerking.

Types of Press

i. Standing Press: use a barbell or dumb-bells.
ii. Press behind neck: use a barbell.
iii. Seated press: use a barbell or dumb-bells.
iv. Seated press behind neck: use a barbell.
v. Press from rack: set the bar at a height suitable for strengthening the arms and shoulders in their weakest zone.
vi. Inclined bench press: set the bench to an angle of at least 60 degrees to the floor. Use a barbell or dumb-bells.
vii. Bench press: use a barbell or dumb-bells. This exercise enables heavy weights to be handled, but care should be taken not to overdo this movement because it is not an overhead movement. However, it can provide variety, as well as resting the other parts of the body while the arms are worked. After bench pressing, perform some overhead arm-stretching movements using straight arms working through as great a range of movement as possible.

Perform 5 sets of 3–5 repetitions. With barbell presses the width of the grip can be varied according to the effect desired. A narrow grip emphasizes the elbow extensor muscles, whereas a wide grip places the load more on the shoulder muscles.

Training Methods

The Clean and Jerk is a lift which takes a great deal of time to master properly. In the early stages of learning coaches should ensure that their pupils spend sufficient time on reiterative practice with relatively light weights. The Clean should be practised separately from the Jerk at first; later they can be added together. Assistance exercises are important at all stages, but beginners should be given plenty of technical assistance work so that skilled movement patterns are reinforced. Skilful, well-timed movements are satisfying to perform and can be more motivating than failures with heavy weights, especially in the early stages.

Advanced lifters are still concerned with technique but to a lesser degree than novices and those of intermediate standard. Peak form in competition is the chief aim of seasoned lifters: this is examined in Chapter 7.

A BEGINNER'S SCHEDULE

The following is based on a top Clean and Jerk of 80 kg (176¼ lb) and should be performed twice a week. This schedule will enable the lifter to progress from an early beginner's stage.

Warm-up: Clean and push Jerk 3 × 5 (light barbell only)
Cleans: 2 × 4—45 kg (99 lb)
2 × 3—52·5 kg (115½ lb)
1 × 2—60 kg (132 lb)
Jerks: sets, reps and poundages as for the Clean
Clean: 4 × 2—52·5 kg (115½ lb)
Assistance exercises: select one or two and perform as described previously.

This beginner's Clean and Jerk may be incorporated into the main training schedule. If possible, the weight should be increased by a small amount every two or three weeks. Perfection of technique should be the objective. On no account should beginners force their poundages. Take a short rest between sets for recovery purposes; do not move to the next set if the breathing rate is high. Train at least three times weekly with workouts lasting from 1½ to 2 hours.

Seven Weightlifting: Advanced Training Methods

Experienced lifters prepare themselves carefully because they wish to win competitions. Carefully planned training programmes, hard work, attention to such details as technique, diet, living habits, psychological approach, avoidance of staleness and other features all play their part in arriving at a peak on a given date. Sound coaching plays an important part too. The coach can set out the general training plan, give specific coaching advice when required, relieve the lifter of much worry and give tactical advice. This and the next chapter will explain these areas.

Training Cycles

The leading weightlifting nations prepare their top lifters through the use of comparatively long-term programmes or macrocycles which are broken down into smaller training cycles or microcycles. These in turn may be divided into phases of preparation. The long-term preparation may take years whereas the training cycle varies between a few months and a year depending upon the competition calendar and the number of peaks aimed at.

An annual plan may provide for two peaks, each leading up to major championships. In this case the year's programme would contain a double cycle. The first cycle would aim at attaining peak form at the National Championships. The second cycle would refer to the build-up of a higher peak form than the first cycle, since it would coincide with more important championships such as the European Championships. Thus the calendar determines the times for peaking up.

Each peak is preceded by a Competitive Period lasting from four to six weeks, which in turn is preceded by a longer Preparatory Period of about three months' duration. These two periods, plus a rest period, sometimes known as the Post-Competitive Period, constitute a full cycle.

Some coaches advocate a yearly cycle with three months' training allocated to each phase, including periods of rest. The Polish team achieved good results a few years ago with a nine months' cycle of three phases, each of which lasted three months—preparation for competition was incorporated into the last month of the third phase. But it is practical to plan in terms of two peaks, each requiring its own cycle, the length of which is determined by the dates of the two main competitions. The cycles are unlikely to be of equal length. Also, the length of the component phases may differ.

Each cycle with its periods may be broken down into the following phases:

Preparatory Period			Com-petition Period	Com-petition peak	Transi-tion Period
phase 1 general preparation	phase 2 strength build-up	phase 3 strength and technique			

Unlike beginners who may use generalized training routines, advanced lifters need to take individual needs into account. The following information on training phases is intended for general guidance. It may be quite impossible for some lifters to train as suggested because of personal commitments.

Planning the training of top lifters is complex since there are so many variables involved. The training plans vary between nations. In addition, the approach varies between coaches and there is a variety of individual differences in the lifters themselves to be considered. However, the following variables are taken into account: long- and short-term cycles; training tonnage; intensity; number of lifts; type of lifts and exercises; percentages of loads for different lifts; number of sets and repetitions; variations of these and other factors; and the practical application of these variables.

Training Cycle Phases

General Preparation

The main aim of this period is to improve the general physical and psychological condition of the lifter. Attention has to be given to the chief parameters of physical fitness discussed in Chapter 2. Specific objectives are the development of stamina, speed, flexibility, power and skill. The development of strength is not accentuated in this phase: it is deferred until the lifter is physically fit. The health, morale and general well-being of the lifter are important also. This phase may last up to one-third of the duration of a major cycle. The type of loading is extensive, so that several exercises are performed, but having a small to medium intensity with relatively short rest pauses. In a workout the lifter should fatigue slowly.

Usually three days a week are given over to general fitness training, which is concentrated on cardiorespiratory efficiency and strength endurance. The following activities are typically employed early in the first phase: repetition sprints of 40 to 60 m alternated with brisk walks of the same distance; circuit training; jumping exercises—vertical and horizontal jumps in multiples of five to ten—performed without resistance at first, then with light dumb-bells; rope skipping—worked up to two minutes non-stop; partner exercises; medicine ball exercises—individually, in pairs and in groups; and team games—non-body-contact such as volleyball and basketball.

Later, short, fairly brisk cross-country runs of 1,000 to 2,000 m performed in woodland and over hilly ground can be introduced. Many lifters find this exhilarating. Three runs a week can help to increase the lifter's physical fitness. In addition, a short swim, a cycle ride, some light athletics or approved team games of a recreative nature should be performed once a week for variety.

Flexibility exercises for the shoulders, spine, hips and ankles should be included in the general preparation. Where a specific joint lacks suppleness, suitable stretching exercises should be practised to increase the joint's range of movement. If possible, progress should be checked by measurement with a modified protractor or goniometer. In other joints, mobility should be maintained.

Barbell training in the early stages of the first phase should be of high repetitions and relatively low intensity. Correct technique should be stressed. Gradual progression is made with strengthening movements for the muscles of the back, legs, abdomen, arms and shoulders. In the early weeks of this phase one lifting session a week is sufficient; it should be changed after a month to six weeks. It is then permissible to train with weights for two light sessions weekly. Separate schedules are used.

An early fitness schedule with weights could be on the following lines. Repetitions should be increased weekly.

Free Squats performed rapidly: 40–50 increasing to 75
'*Good morning' exercise* with very light barbell: 12
Vertical jumps with very light barbell: 2 × 10
Snatch with light barbell: 2 × 10
Front squats or lunges: 15 reps increasing to 25
Snatches without foot movement or dip: 12–15 reps increasing to 25
Abdominal raise: 15 reps increasing to 30

Alternating schedules for systematic progression in the later stages of this first phase could be on the following lines. These are not intended to be rigid, but should be thought of as flexible and variable according to the individual lifter's needs.

SCHEDULE A
Warm-up
Prone hyperextension: 3 × 10 reps
Snatch balance: 4 × 5 reps
Jerk: 5 × 3 reps
Clean pulls: 5 × 5 reps
Front Squats or lunges: 3 × 8 reps
Inclined sit-up: 3 × 10 reps
Mobility exercises: 5 minutes

SCHEDULE B
Warm-up
'Good morning' exercise: 3 × 10 reps
Snatch: 5 × 3 reps
Power Clean: 3 × 8 reps
Jerk balance: 3 × 5 reps
Snatch pulls: 5 × 5 reps
Jump Squats: 3 × 8 reps
Mobility exercises: 5 minutes

Schedule A should be performed on days 1 and 3, Schedule B on days 2 and 4, and so on.

It will be seen that in the early stages of the general preparation, a typical week's training is composed of three days' fitness work selected from an array of conditioning activities, one day's barbell training and one day's recreative exercise. Later, this may be changed to two days' fitness training, two days' barbell work and one day's recreative exercises. But these are only guidelines. All training should be recorded in the lifter's training diary.

If possible, medical checks should be made at the beginning of the first phase and then at regular intervals. At the end of this phase the lifter should be physically fit, possess an enhanced feeling of well-being and the ability to recover quickly after exercise. He should have at least a week's 'active rest' at the end of this phase. This general preparation is the foundation for the heavier strengthening work of the next phase.

STRENGTH BUILD-UP

The main aim of the second phase is to build up muscular strength through the regular use of heavy weights. The high repetitions with light weights change to lower repetitions with heavier intensity. Fitness exercises are continued throughout this phase. Because of the fast nature of the two competitive lifts, speed is stressed.

Usually the length of this phase lasts up to one-third of the duration of the complete cycle, but it may be varied according to the requirements of the lifter. Since strength is such an important quality for a weightlifter, the length of this phase may be arranged to make it the longest phase, depending on the lifting calendar and the needs of the lifter.

The Hungarian split workout, consisting of two schedules practised alternately, is popular. Moreover, the idea can be adopted for those who, for various reasons such as work commitments, travelling, and limited energy, cannot train under ideal conditions. Each schedule contains five or six exercises, including two lifts and assistance exercises. The Clean and Jerk is usually treated as two separate lifts for training purposes. Typical assistance exercises are Snatch and Clean pulls, Squats or lunges, 'good morning' exercises, power Cleans, power Snatches and so forth. Speed, fitness and flexibility exercises are continued since the weightlifter's strength cannot be applied properly if quickness, the ability to recover rapidly, and mobility are neglected.

The Hungarian method uses up to 7 sets of 5 repetitions with most exercises. Prone hyperextensions and 'good morning' exercises are best performed for 3 sets of 10 repetitions. Hard work and regularity of training are important. Four workouts a week are the absolute minimum; five or six are better. With four workouts weekly the lifter has three days' rest; with six he has but one. In certain cases a different training schedule is used for each workout. It is repeated on the corresponding workout the following week.

The first week's training load is light. It is increased in the second week. Then it is decreased in the third week for recovery purposes. In the fourth week a larger increase is applied. The next week is light, and so on.

The Russian training principle of alternating light, medium and heavy loads can be applied to each predetermined spell of training, which may be within the week, weekly, fortnightly, three-weekly or monthly. Of course, the discretion of the coach is necessary when working out a plan. As a general guide, the following percentages of the best lifts are calculated in order to classify loads: light, 60–70 per cent; medium, 70–80 per cent; heavy, 80–90 per cent. The coach may wish to vary the tonnage and intensity according to the dates of competitions and his knowledge of the lifter. But increases in training loads are generally made because the best lifts improve. However, light spells should be used for recuperation.

In a personal interview with Falameev, the following lifts, expressed as percentages of the monthly training load, were suggested as a basis for good lifters:

Snatch: 26 per cent
Jerk: 25 per cent
Snatch pulls: 8–10 per cent
Clean pulls: 6–8 per cent
Pressing movements: 10 per cent
Squatting movements: 23–26 per cent

The use of relatively light weights for dynamic training was stressed. For 50 per cent of the planned training lifts it was reported that 67–77 per cent of best results should be used.

Very heavy loads cannot be sustained for long periods without staleness occurring, so variations in tonnage and intensities have to be applied to both individual training sessions and weekly spells. Careful observation and common sense should be employed when deciding on these variations. A general training routine applicable to all lifters does not exist for all top-class lifters since their individual needs and circumstances vary. Many lifters drain their reserves by training with too great a weight. Thus several successful training plans are needed, not only alternate loads on a weekly basis but also for individual workouts. In general, heavy training, whether for the week or a single session, is followed by a light session to ensure recovery.

In the middle of this phase sometimes a variation in training is used. For example the lifter may be fit and strong, and able to train six days weekly, with rest taken on the seventh. He may have a different training schedule each day with alternating loads, together with weekly tonnage variations. Repetitions range from 3 to 5, with higher repetitions for back and light conditioning exercises. The following is an example of this type of training.

	1st week	*2nd week*
Monday	Schedule A—light	Schedule A—light
Tuesday	Schedule B—medium	Schedule B—heavy
Wednesday	Schedule C—light	Schedule C—light
Thursday	Schedule D—medium	Schedule D—heavy
Friday	Schedule E—light	Schedule E—light
Saturday	Schedule F—medium	Schedule F—heavy
Sunday	rest	rest

The third and fourth weeks would follow a similar pattern but the overall intensity would be slightly higher.

The light sessions are used for speed and the heavier ones for exercises such as Squats or pulls.

Where a lifter trains four times a week, if possible, he would train for two days, rest a day, train for two days, then rest for two days. Where he trains five times a week, he would normally train for three days, rest a day, train two days, rest a day or exercise lightly on the 'active rest' principle.

In the later stages of the second phase, increased practice for technique occurs. This is with heavy weights. Faults may have to be eliminated. Repetitions are kept to 5 or lower, sometimes using a 5, 4, 3, 2, 1 pyramid basis, finishing with several singles. Workouts should finish with five to six minutes' running, stretching and free exercises of a massive nature to help oxidize fatigue products and maintain muscle elasticity. Then a hot shower lasting four or five minutes, followed by a brisk towelling down, will be found to be beneficial. A week's 'active rest' is taken at the end of this phase.

Strength and Technique

The aim in this phase is to achieve technical form in the two lifts while retaining the strength developed in the previous phase.

The development of speed is stressed. The major part of training is composed of the Snatch, and the Clean and Jerk. Assistance exercises should bear some relationship to the movement patterns of the competitive lifts. Positive transfer of training is an important objective with every movement geared to correct stereotyping of technique. Suitable assistance exercises are snatch and clean pulls, heavy balance exercises and the technical assistance exercises already described in this book. In addition, back exercises and explosive jumps are continued.

Not only do technical faults have to be eradicated entirely, but both mind and body have to become accustomed to the heavier training and fighting to keep lifts in the groove. The lifter becomes mentally tougher. The training volume is decreased and intensity increased. While tonnage is important, it is secondary to intensity. Pyramid progression, working up to heavy singles on the two lifts, is applied at least every fortnight.

Near the end of this phase, some lifters who rely mainly on power have used with success two alternating schedules, one medium and one heavy in load. Repetitions are either fives or threes. The training extends into the final competition phase. At the start the load is at least 70 per cent, working up to 100 per cent just before the competition, when the lifter tapers off.

The conservation of energy of the lifter must be watched in this phase. The distribution of effort on heavy-intensity movements differs from those of light-intensity. The lifter has to concentrate more and will find a heightened kinaesthetic sense an advantage. It becomes a difficult task for the coach if the lifter cannot get hold of the correct 'feel' with heavy weights. Passive recreation in a pleasant atmosphere can do much to alleviate the effects of the stress of this phase. Walks in the park, visits to the theatre, games of cards or chess are all restful for the nervous system. The coach must not be afraid to reduce both tonnage and intensity for a few workouts if there is evidence of staleness.

Competition Preparation

This is the shortest phase of all and is an extension of the previous phase. In fact some leading coaches believe it to be an integral part of that phase. It refers to that period of about thirty to forty days before a major competition. On the big day the lifter has to be on peak form ready to produce his explosive best while discharging all his stored up energy.

Any mistakes made in previous training should be noted and not repeated. For example, fatigue may have been caused previously because heavy Squats were used too near the competition date. Normally they should be omitted about a fortnight beforehand. The number of exercises, sets and repetitions in a workout will depend on the lifter's fitness, experience and ability to tolerate high-intensity workouts.

The intensity of training weights is increased progressively from the beginning of this period of preparation. Maximum intensity is reached seven to ten days before the competition. The first fortnight employs tonnages progressing from light to medium, using medium-intensity weights. The third week is concerned with heavy-intensity: tonnage is reduced and workouts are shortened. About a fortnight before the competition, starting poundages may be used for the Clean and Jerk. After that the lifter tapers off, reducing training, cutting out assistance exercises likely to cause fatigue, and taking more rest of various kinds. Then follows one brief training session a day on the Snatch and the Clean and Jerk, alternated with a day's rest. On the penultimate workout, the lifter works up to the starting poundage on the Snatch. The last workout is light and is taken three days before the competition. The last two days before a competition are for complete rest. Passive recreation on rest days is of paramount importance. Some top lifters use different plans, decreasing intensity and tonnage a fortnight to a month before the main competition.

As a guide to tonnage and intensity in the competitive phase, some coaches calculate a Coefficient of Intensity (CI). This is derived from the Average Intensity (AI) of a previous thirty-day training period. The CI is simply the previous AI divided by the last total achieved for the two lifts, expressed as a percentage. A new AI can be found by multiplying the CI by the new total aimed for and dividing by 100. This will give the extra intensity to work for in the new training period. The new tonnage is found by multiplying the new AI by the old tonnage. With this method, the lifter is concerned with the increased intensity. Also, the new total aimed for must be realistic.

After the second competition peak the lifter needs to be refreshed and to do something different from lifting. Accordingly he should take a month's 'active rest', of which the first week or two is complete rest. Then light free-conditioning exercises and gentle physical recreation of a non-body-contact variety can be carried out. In the following year a 10 per cent increase in tonnage is aimed for, but this depends on how hard the lifter can train.

Reducing Bodyweight

Care should be taken when reducing in order to 'make the weight' for a given category. In particular, youths should not be expected to dry out too much nor too frequently. A restriction of fluid in order to lose weight can be dangerous since curtailment of fluid may result in liver and kidney damage. Youths need a minimum of 1½ litres (2⅝ pints) of fluid daily. Also, growing youths need adequate nourishment. Light, easily digestible meals are required before a competition. Complete starvation is not recommended because there is a danger of waste products being collected in the body rather than eliminated. It should be noted that more waste products are eliminated with fluids than with solids. With growing lifters, it may be wise to build up their bodyweight into a higher category rather than risk unhealthy complications. Sometimes lifters move up more than one class. Common sense has to be used regarding the desirability of reduction.

To lose weight most lifters reduce the high-energy foods in their normal diet for a day or two, plus a reduction of fluid and salt. In some cases, weight has to be lost over a period of several days. Experience has to be gained regarding the period of reduction, the amount of food and drink, and perspiration-inducing activity.

Bodyweight reductions by sweating are in order for losing up to 2 kg (4½ lb). To lose a minute amount of weight the lifter wears lots of clothing and performs leg exercises such as free squats, running and skipping. For larger amounts of weight reduction a hot bath or sauna is taken and then the lifter is wrapped in towels and blankets to absorb the sweat. The heating of the body should last about one-third of the time required for resting and perspiring. A quarter of an hour in a sauna followed by three-quarters of an hour in a blanket reduces bodyweight by about 600 g (19 oz).

Once the lifter has weighed in he may take a couple of glasses of fluid such as lemon tea, but pure water should be avoided because of the possibility of cramp. He may take a meal consisting of lightly boiled eggs, chicken and chicken soup. Salt should be replaced. Some lifters claim that two or three 100 mg tablets of ascorbic acid are beneficial.

The prolonged use of sauna or Turkish baths to reduce bodyweight is inadvisable. To lose too much weight by excessive sweating immediately before a contest is also undesirable and should be avoided. Lifters may become weakened due to the loss of body fluid and salt. Also, there is a risk of cramp. However, some lifters do not experience adverse effects by taking no liquid on the day of the event right up to the weigh-in. Some coaches administer diuretic substances such as Navidex which cause urination. In such cases it is important to replace the water-retention factors (sodium and potassium) after the weigh-in, especially potassium.

There are individual differences in reducing: some find it easy, others difficult and tiring. A loss of 2 kg ($4\frac{1}{2}$ lb) may not affect a 110 kg lifter but it can have serious consequences for one of 52 kg.

Warming-up

The stimulating activity known as the warm-up consists of general and specific activities performed for a few minutes before the actual lifting starts in order to prepare the lifter physiologically and psychologically for the effort of competition. The idea is to warm up all the muscles generally with free exercises, then move to full-range exercises and shadow lifting before using light barbell movements. Central warming up and increased peripheral blood-flow must be obtained. Then progressive increases in the barbell's intensity are made, working up to or near to the proposed starting poundages. The warm-up is effective when carried out right up to the time when a lifter's name is called to lift. Warming up followed by a long pause before lifting loses its effect. Between lifts, a lifter must continue to keep warm with shadow and barbell movements. He must keep warm throughout the competition.

Lifting heavy weights demands a great intake of oxygen which is provided by faster, deeper and more economical respiration, together with increased circulation. A greater blood supply is required by the lifter's muscles, which are less likely to be injured if they are warm. Suitable movements can augment the lifter's regulating mechanism; gradual, active body movements which do not exhaust him are useful. These movements are of an individual nature, and they cause the lifter to feel that his muscles are warm and ready to lift. He must warm up in his track suit to conserve heat.

Stretching exercises relate to the lifting movements. They enable any slight stiffness to be eliminated and possibly reinforce kinaesthesis. Shadow lifting helps co-ordination and may be used to make the lifter think about what he is doing. Barbell warming up is more purposeful and progressive. A light barbell is used at first, then the weights are increased. The lifter has to continue to warm up for each attempt as it comes and he should not cool down. It is advisable to wear a track suit between lifts. Too much sitting around should be avoided. Also, avoidance of cold draughts is important.

The last training phase before the competition will give the lifter an opportunity to establish some idea of starting poundages besides suitable warm-up activities and increments on the barbell. At the end of the warm-up and later stages, the lifter's state of mind as well as his body is important. He should have confidence in himself, a sense of purpose, concentration and the will to win. Careful warming up, continued throughout the competition, can have a motivating effect.

Here is an example of a warm-up.

1. *General:* running on the spot, skipping, rhythmic jumping and free exercises for all muscle groups. This section must not be too extensive.
   3 minutes.
2. *Stretching:* gentle, full-range movements for the joints of the ankles, knees, hips, spine and shoulders. Also, any stiff muscles should be stretched.
   2–3 minutes.
3. *Shadow lifting:* rehearse movement patterns of the lifts.
   2–3 minutes.
4. *Barbell:* start light with singles using about 40 per cent of the best lift. Continue to use singles with increased intensity working to 10 kg (22 lb) below starting weight. Then perform 2 reps with starting weight on pull only.
   10–12 minutes.
5. Repeat the fourth stage when required during the contest, but usually working up to 90 per cent of the starting poundage. Aim to be warm just before each attempt, without reducing working capacity.

Starting Poundages

The competition training phase will indicate the lifter's best performance on the Snatch and the Clean and Jerk. Careful preparation will ensure that the lifter is fresh and that he does not leave his best lifting in the gymnasium; but the temperament of the lifter, the competition environment and the attitude of the coach are influencing variables here.

With relatively inexperienced competitors, it is advisable to start with 5 kg (11 lb) below his best. If successful, his second attempt would equal his previous best, with his third attempt reserved for a new personal best. If his placing can be improved by taking a little more and he is rising to the occasion, then a realistic increase would be in order. Abject failures can be harmful in many ways.

The prime objectives of experienced competitors are winning or placing high, or beating a previous best total. Selection of poundages becomes complex, and relates to the strength of the opposition, the way the competition is going, competition stimulus, previous training, the lifting environment and so on. Tactics, luck and experience are involved. However, a successful first attempt, which should be neither too high nor too low, can elevate a lifter's spirits into the right mood for subsequent lifts. A failure or failures can be demoralizing. Three failures on a lift mean elimination from the contest. The lifter should not have to worry about starting poundages as this is the job of the coach, who has to assess the situation carefully and then choose responsibly. The lifter has to respond as positively as possible.

If, despite thorough planning and good intentions, things go wrong, the situation should be evaluated and treated as a lesson learned for the future.

Eight Lifting: Other Factors Affecting Performance

Staleness, bad living habits, a faulty diet, a wrong psychological attitude and other factors can seriously affect a lifter's training and his competition results. Doping can elevate performance but it is unfair and forbidden. Some of the more important issues are considered below.

Staleness

Training causes fatigue with a temporary drop in the efficiency of the lifter. After a suitable period of time, the lifter recovers his efficiency. The application of training volume and intensity, rest pauses between sets, length of workout, spacing of workouts and rest of various kinds are all aimed at increasing the lifter's efficiency. However, accumulated fatigue can occur as a result of overtraining: this and other factors produce a drop in performance. This is sometimes referred to as staleness.

Coaches must be vigilant of staleness and try to prevent it. According to Kereszty, staleness may be the result of the following causes: overtraining, overexertion, fitness deficiencies and external disturbing factors.

Overtraining originates mainly in the nervous system and should not occur if the training is correctly conducted. It can be avoided by gradual progression and sufficient variety in the training programme. If there is excess fatigue following training, it may be due to overtraining. It can affect the lifter's confidence as well as making him irritable and nervous. It should be checked by cutting back on the training load and by the application of rest. An overtrained lifter just cannot produce the extra effort demanded in competition.

Overexertion arises when the lifter is subjected to great load without adequate preparation. Such 'forcing' can cause deviations in the heart. It can occur after prolonged illness also. Staleness due to overexertion is serious; the lifter should be referred to a doctor. Fortunately, such cases are rare, but complete rest and medical treatment seems to be the only cure. Extra care should be taken with young lifters and novices.

Unbalanced fitness training can give rise to fitness deficiencies. Also these can arise out of hidden illness such as influenza which affects the lifter's state of health. However, improper living is the real culprit. Symptoms are poor sleep, fatigue and weight loss. If these persist, the lifter should see his doctor.

External disturbing factors may be due to unfamiliar food and water, travelling effects, changes in the weather and tension between the lifter and others. Conflict between the lifter and his team-mates or the coach can disturb the lifter's performance. The coach has to be tactful, especially just before a competition.

It is the coach's duty to prevent staleness. One aid is to end each workout with five or six minutes of moderate activity comprising varied running and free exercise. Not only does this help to remove fatigue products but it has been found to help the heart and blood pressure to recover more quickly. This has been labelled 'recovery training'. The use of a hand dynamometer to test grip strength is a useful aid: if a lifter cannot grip as much as usual on a 'heavy' training night, he lowers his training load and barbell intensity.

When a coach has to overcome a mild case of staleness, he should reduce the training load. It may be necessary to change the schedule. The lifter's diet should be checked and the vitamin intake increased if necessary. Where a lifter's bodyweight is low, a high-energy diet plus plenty of protein helps. Warm baths and tonic medicines sometimes help. Debilitating habits should be avoided.

Smoking

Tobacco is best avoided altogether. One cigarette effectively reduces the haemoglobin in the blood by 8 per cent. Since haemoglobin carries the oxygen in the blood and since oxygen is necessary for physical and mental effort, it is obvious that smoking will affect athletic performance. Moreover, cigarette smoking is potentially disastrous to one's health. There is a relationship between cigarette smoking and lung cancer. Smoking can lead to vitamin neutralization or depletion, in particular of vitamins A, B1, B6, B12, C and pantothenic acid. Smoking decreases the size of blood vessels, thereby contributing to high blood-pressure.

Alcohol

Alcohol is a narcotic and too much can be dangerous. It is not a stimulant. It causes loss of efficiency: it does not help endurance because it slows down the removal of lactic acid—the fatigue product caused by exercise. Too much alcohol, especially the strong spirits, not only dulls the nervous system, but over a period of time can depress both the mind and the body. The lifter should avoid strong alcohol because it upsets the nervous system: it dehydrates essential moisture in the body, thereby affecting the proper functioning of nerves. It affects clear thinking and interferes with neuromuscular co-ordination. However, if it is taken in moderation and certainly not within forty-eight hours of a contest, it is possible to maintain a fairly high standard of performance. A little wine taken with a meal or a beer after training may be good for morale. Spirits taken regularly are not acceptable.

Diet

A lifter needs a balanced diet of good, wholesome food. The three essential foodstuffs are carbohydrate, protein and fat. Carbohydrates provide energy; proteins maintain, repair and build tissues; while fats provide energy in a concentrated form as well as body insulation. The body also needs water, minerals, vitamins and microelements such as cobalt and manganese. A lifter must have adequate nutrition and sufficient fluids for his needs. Varied, attractive, nourishing food in the correct amount is a step in the right direction towards an adequate diet. Moreover, variety of food promotes better assimilation.

'Complete' proteins containing essential amino acids, which are required for the muscles and the blood, should be eaten at each meal. Animal proteins such as eggs, milk, cheese, fish, meat and poultry are complete proteins. Cereal and vegetable proteins are incomplete, but are used in balancing the diet. At least half the lifter's protein intake should consist of complete or first-class protein in order to repair or build up new tissues. Meat is particularly beneficial. Foods of animal origin are valuable for their mineral substances.

Carbohydrates are sugars and starches of various kinds. The amount required varies according to the lifter's individual needs. The greater his physical output, the greater is his requirement of energy foods. The best guide to the amount of carbohydrates is bodyweight: if too much is taken, bodyweight will increase and vice versa. The same will apply to some of the protein intake, but it is not as significant as carbohydrate or fat as a source of energy. When a competition is imminent, the intake of energy foods is increased, unless the lifter has to reduce. Pre-contest meals should not consist of meat, fish or eggs since protein is almost useless at that stage. The lifter wants easily assimilated starch and, therefore, foods such as cereals especially porridge, macaroni, raisins, honey and glucose are appropriate.

On average the lifter utilizes 15 g (0·527 oz) of food in the following proportions for each kg (2·2 lb) of his bodyweight: 16 per cent protein; 14 per cent fat; and 70 per cent carbohydrate. An additional 10 per cent is usually added to these requirements when calculating raw food because of losses in cooking, preparation and incomplete assimilation. This is equivalent to 80 dietetic calories of food for each kg of the lifter's bodyweight. A middleweight lifter weighing 75 kg (165 lb) needs about 5,000 calories or 1,200 g (42 oz) of food. If this is too much, bodyweight will go up; if too little, it will decrease. The food intake should be adjusted accordingly: input and output must be balanced. However, it is permissible for the lifter to be a little overweight for training purposes. For a 75 kg lifter, protein intake should not exceed 200 g (7 oz) a day since acids and other substances difficult to eliminate may be retained in the system.

Since water is constantly lost from the body in exhaled air, sweat, urine and in the faeces, it must be replaced if health is to be maintained. Salt, which contains the water-retention factor—sodium, must be replaced also.

Mineral and vitamin requirements are met in a balanced diet. Fresh green vegetables, animal fat, wholemeal bread, milk and milk products such as cheese will meet most mineral and vitamin requirements.

Vitamin capsules, wheat-germ oil, iron tablets and powdered protein are popular dietary supplements among lifters. However, an average mixed diet should contain sufficient minerals and vitamins for normal training. If health or fitness is affected, or some of the foods eaten are grown in poor soil, or a person is unable to absorb natural vitamins, it may be necessary to prescribe vitamin pills or other dietary supplements. During hard training, vitamins are important in the lifter's diet. Falameev recommends the following daily doses: C, 50 mg; B1, 2–10 mg; B6, 3–4 mg; B12, 10 mg; PP, 15–30 mg; A, up to 5 mg; E, up to 10 mg.

Personal Hygiene

Physical fitness does not render a lifter immune from disease. He has to take basic precautions to preserve his health. A lifter has to pay attention to his toilet habits, cleanliness, dental care, sex and other health considerations.

Regular bowel habits are desirable; these can often be cultivated by toilet training. 'Nature's call' should not be ignored. Adequate dietary fibre is necessary and may be obtained by regularly taking wholemeal products or millers' bran, which is sold in health food stores. If a lifter is constipated he should not practise dubious forms of self-medication but should see a doctor. Heavily spiced food can cause frequent urination.

A lifter should keep himself scrupulously clean. He should take a warm, tepid shower after each workout to get rid of perspiration. This should be followed by careful drying, especially in the skin folds and between the toes. A lifter should ensure that his socks, lifting costume, support and track suit are washed regularly.

Care of the mouth and teeth is important. In addition to elementary dental hygiene, regular visits to the dentist should be arranged. It should be noted that there is a connection between dental sepsis and muscle injury.

Normal sexual activity will not weaken a lifter. It can be stimulating and invigorating. The main point for the lifter to note is that established patterns of sexual behaviour with one's partner are not harmful. The normal pattern does not require changing because an important competition is near. Extra-marital intercourse is a controversial area. It is complicated because of social and psychological factors, and is a personal matter involving moral judgements.

Many lifters do not get enough fresh air. For good respiratory hygiene, warm, clean and moist air is required. Many gymnasia are cold, dusty and dry; if these undesirable features cannot be remedied, a change of training quarters is suggested. Walks in the fresh air are pleasant and healthy and can be used to advantage by the lifter.

Some lifters ruin advanced training through worry, insufficient sleep and catching colds. They should try to maintain a tranquil mind—if an overambitious training programme causes anxiety, it should be rewritten in more realistic terms. Late nights, irregular hours and uncomfortable beds or surroundings may have to be remedied. When training with a heavy tonnage, sleep simply cannot be skimped. Most lifters require eight to nine hours' sleep nightly.

Lifters should not train if they have a cold; rather they should keep at an even temperature and rest. Those susceptible to colds may find bacterial cold vaccines effective, but they do not work for everybody. It is important to wear a track suit in most climates since local chilling easily occurs during the rest pauses between sets of exercises. Dress should be appropriate to the weather—this is a matter of common sense. Vitamin A deficiency and excessive fatigue increase the risk of catching cold.

Doping

In some cases, doping is carried out to increase artificially and unfairly a lifter's performance. Drugs are usually prescribed by doctors and are not normally found in the diet.

Pharmaceutical aids are used by some lifters. Stimulant drugs such as amphetamines and other forms of dope are expressly forbidden by the I.W.F. which tries to control their use by dope tests. Those found using any of the forbidden drugs are disqualified from competition and suspended from further competition for a period decided by the I.W.F. Bureau.

In recent years, anabolic steroids have been taken by some lifters. These have been nicknamed 'fertilizers' or 'bulk bombs'. They are taken in order to compete on equal terms with others. Apart from the moral issue of cheating, indiscriminate use of certain steroids can affect the reproductive organs and cause liver damage, according to some authorities. Although subject to individual variations, there is a risk of atrophy, or wastage of the genitalia due to loss of production of the male sex hormone, testosterone. Another claim is that large doses taken over a long period will lead to adrenal gland suppression. However, non-hormonal anabolic substances produce fewer side effects; but not enough is known of the hazards, dosage and the influence on youths who are not fully grown. Most members of the medical profession deplore the use of anabolic steroids for sport purposes.

The lifter and coach may be tempted in this respect and their position is a difficult one. It is a fact that being artificially overweight has a negative effect on locomotor activity. The strength/bodyweight ratio decreases as the lifters become heavier. Moreover, there is a test for anabolic steroids and this is now used by the I.W.F. But some lifters still use these substances for a period, and then discontinue their use several weeks before a competition. Kereszti has stated that such substances can be effective for athletes who are tired or have a negative nitrogen balance. No doubt the debate will continue as well as the illegal use of these drugs. But their use cannot be condoned, because they are prohibited by the I.W.F. and there are risks besides.

The use of drugs is a serious problem, of course, to weightlifting authorities and the medical profession. The I.W.F. lists the following groups of forbidden doping substances: psychomotor drugs, sympathomimetic amines, various central nervous system stimulants, narcotic analgesics and anabolic steroids. In major competitions lifters in the first three places and one other drawn at random may be tested. This is one way of anti-doping control.

Injuries

The coach should try to prevent injuries. Sports' medicine authorities suggest that 85–90 per cent of injuries are preventable. Attention to physical fitness, sound technique, warming up, mobilizing, avoidance of 'forcing' methods, balanced development of physique, insistence on appropriate equipment, boots and clothing, avoidance of congested or draughty training quarters, checking for slippery platforms and insistence on the use of collars all help to reduce the risk of injury.

Muscle strains, ligament sprains and swellings and other injuries do occur sometimes. These matters are for the doctor. If there is delay in getting an injured lifter to hospital or to a doctor, apply cold (in the form of ice) to the injury which should be kept above the level of the heart to prevent swelling.

Psychological Factors

The level of a lifter's performance depends not only on physical preparation but also on psychological factors. Both the lifter and the coach are concerned with the psychology of lifting. Each has his own unique personality. The sport has its own set of rules, competition tensions, uncertainties, tactics and gamesmanship which affect contest psychology.

The coach has to motivate the lifter and continue to stimulate him at the right time. Overmotivation too early during the day of the competition can cause pre-match nerves which can change to apathy and depressed performance. Knowledge, experience and intuition enable the coach to time the stimulation of the lifter. Much depends on the relationship between the coach and the lifter.

For example, the coach can induce the lifter into a state of slight excitement by making positive comments. If the lifter is phlegmatic, he needs stirring up a little. If overexcitement is noticed, he needs calming down by conversation directed towards certainty and confidence, perhaps by reinforcing memories of past success. Lifters differ in their attitudes regarding their opponents. Some want to know the form of their opponent, while timorous ones shy away from such discussion. The coach must act in accordance with the lifter's attitude. For example, introverts are best left alone, while extroverts can be occupied with conversation on suitable topics.

The nervous system of a lifter becomes more tense in the last two or three days before a competition, especially if he has to reduce his bodyweight. Distraction from outside stimuli can help to soothe and protect a lifter's nerves. Gentle recreation by way of walking in pleasant surroundings, a visit to the theatre or cinema, lectures, listening to classical music, games of chess or cards and discussions on non-lifting subjects can be beneficial.

Motivation is behaviour based on needs and directed towards goals. Some lifters need to prove themselves in the eyes of the world. Their goals are lifting a particular weight or winning a Championship in order to demonstrate their prowess. Having done so, the lifter is gratified for a while, then another motivation cycle is set up, often with higher goals. Much depends on the lifter's ego, need of fame, national or religious pride, compensation for failure or fear of being labelled inadequate. At the appropriate stage, high goals such as the requirements for national squad selection and high qualifying totals for major competitions, can do much to raise standards. When a lifter fails to reach his goal, the coach has to be supportive and prevent the lifter from becoming too depressed; he has to analyse the reasons for mistakes and apply what has been learned in setting new goals. Confidence must not be undermined. The coach has to take the blame for wrong tactics, wrong choice of poundages and so on rather than leave the lifter too low. Sometimes the coach has driven his lifter too much;

at other times it may be too little. Careful judgement and a trusting relationship has to develop in order to augment motivation in the best way possible. The use of praise and constructive comments can positively reinforce the right sort of attitude. The lifter must be made to believe in himself and his ability.

Where a team is involved, confidence and being at ease can do much to undermine opposing teams who may become jittery if they assume all is well with the other team. The lighter lifters in a team who compete in the early days of a tournament can do much for team spirit if they perform well. Winning is best, but achieving a personal record suggests that the previous preparation was right.

Before the competition, a lifter should be acquainted with the venue. He should not be distracted by strange surroundings and equipment. Personal details such as clothing, boots, belts, bandages and the use of smelling salts should be checked before the competition. Moreover, a coach must know what is going on in the lifting environment if he is to serve his lifters in the best way.

After suitable motivation the lifter goes on to the platform for an all-out effort. He has to be steamed up, he has to concentrate on the correct movement sequence and discharge his energies in one explosive lift on the Snatch, and in two great efforts on the Clean and Jerk. A positive businesslike approach to the bar works well for most people. Copying the idiosyncrasies and frills of a few top lifters is usually unnecessary—in fact such preliminary behaviour can affect concentration and will inhibit the majority of lifters. The lifter, assisted by his coach, has to make up his mind that he can do the lift. He should be well versed in purposeful platform drill to get on with the lift without hurrying and without too much delay. Much depends on his frame of mind.

Nine Powerlifting: Deep Knees' Bend (Squat)

The Deep Knees' Bend or Squat is a test of leg and hip strength. It is regarded as a key exercise by many people who use weights. Some famous Olympic lifters such as Basanowsky employed the Squat as a general strengthener of the hip and knee extensors. When used with high repetitions it has a beneficial effect on metabolism and the cardio-respiratory processes.

Not only is the Squat used to develop large areas of muscle, but it is also the first of the competitive power lifts. Some of the World records in this lift exceed four times the lifter's own bodyweight. Paul Anderson of the U.S.A. unofficially squatted with a little under 545 kg (1,200 lb). Although the technique is uncomplicated, it must be sound; and training must be sensible.

There are two styles of Squat. The one advocated here uses a flat back. The other style is not recommended generally because it employs a rounded back, which may predispose the lifter towards injury of the spine.

International Rules

The I.P.F. rules state:

1. The lifter must assume an upright position with the top of the bar not more than one inch below the top of the deltoids, the bar across the shoulders in a horizontal position, hands gripping the bar, feet flat on the platform. The use of a wedge at the heels or toes shall be forbidden. Upon removing the bar from the racks, the lifter must move backward to establish his position. He shall wait in this position for the referee's signal, which shall be given as soon as the lifter is motionless and the bar is properly positioned.
2. After the referee's signal, the lifter shall bend the knees and lower the body until the tops of the thighs are below parallel with the platform. The lifter shall recover at will, without double bouncing, to an upright position, knees locked, and wait for the referee's signal to replace the bar, which shall be given when the lifter is absolutely motionless. The lifter shall make a bona fide attempt to return the bar to the rack. The tops of the thighs shall be defined as being the point at the hip joint that bends when the body is lowered. This point shall develop a parallel relationship with the top of the knee. This refers to the surface of the leg at the hip joint that bends when the body is lowered.

3. The apparatus shall be of I.P.F. standards. Padding may be applied to the bar only, but it must not exceed 30 cm ($11\frac{25}{32}$ in) in width and 5 cm ($1\frac{31}{32}$ in) in thickness. The lifter shall remove the bar from the racks, preparatory to the lift.
4. The lifter must face the front of the platform.
5. The lifter may not hold the collars, sleeves or plates, at any time during the performance of the lift. However, the side of the hand may contact the inside of the inner collars.

Causes for Disqualification

a. During the lift, failure to wait for the referee's signals.
b. Any change of the position of the hands on the bar.
c. More than one recovery attempt.
d. Failure to assume an upright position at the start and completion of the lift.
e. Failure to lower the body until the tops of the thighs are below parallel.
f. Any shifting of the feet during the performance of the lift.
g. Any shifting of the bar on the body during the performance of the lift.
h. Any touching of the bar by the spotters (loaders) before the referee's signal.
i. Any raising of the toes or heels.
j. Any touching of the legs with the elbows or upper arms.

Technique of the Squat

Preparation

a. The lifter carefully takes the bar from the squat stands. His feet are placed under the bar, hip width apart. His back is flat and inclined slightly forward. A firm grip is taken, with the hands spaced approximately 15–30 cm (6–12 in) wider than the shoulders. The bar rests just above the shoulder blades, with the trapezius muscles providing a padding against the pressure of heavy weights.
b. The head is erect, the eyes looking forward, and the back muscles contracted throughout their entire length. A deep breath is taken through the mouth. The knees and hips are extended simultaneously to lift the bar upward and off the squat stands.
c. One short step is taken backward so as to clear the stands. The lifter then exhales and takes up the correct starting position.

Starting Position

a. The feet are placed on the same line. The heels are placed approximately hip-width apart, with the toes pointing slightly outward. CAUTION: the wide-legged style of squatting is not recommended because it predisposes towards sprains of the hip and knee ligaments.

b. The shoulders are braced back and the back is kept flat in readiness for the referee's signal which is given when the lifter is motionless and in conformity with the first rule already stated.

c. When the referee signals, a large inhalation through the mouth is recommended. Then follows a controlled descent with head up and hips out so as to prevent the spine from rounding. The chin is kept in to keep the posterior spinal ligaments taut. The hips are outside the base of support and the shoulders are above the knees. The tops of the lifter's thighs must go just below a level parallel with the platform. Control and balance are important at this crucial stage since the direction of movement has to be changed. The hips must be kept level. The feet resist the downward pressure. The knees must point in the direction of the feet. The angles of the back and thighs depend on the relative lengths of those weight arms, which are at their maximum leverage. These principal weight arms receive force from the large extensors of the hips and knees to overcome the weight of the bar, lifter and internal resistance. 'Bouncing' is forbidden.

RECOVERY

a. The lifter continues to drive his feet forcefully into the platform. First the hips drive upward. Then follows a simultaneous push of the quadriceps muscles of the thighs and gluteal muscles of the hips.

b. The hips are then eased forward under the bar. The hips have to travel further forward than the backward excursion of the knees. Thus the knees move back slightly. It is here that a 'sticking point' can occur and the lifter must fight to keep the bar moving. The back muscles are contracted to keep a flat or extended back. The hands and the arms push upward on the bar.

c. Exhale forcefully as the hips move forward. The hip action should not be too vigorous or jerky, since the lifter can be thrown off balance at this juncture.

FIGURE 8. Sequence of movement of the Squat

d. The lifter must finish in an upright position, with knees, hips and shoulders in line, when usually he takes in another breath. Throughout the lift, the hand and foot positions must remain unchanged, with the lifter looking to his front.

Remarks

The preceding standard technique is recommended because it is safe. However, individual lifters may vary certain aspects of it. For example, the feet may be parallel, especially if the knee drive seems inadequate. Some squatters use a wider stance.

Many lifters use heels on their boots when performing the Squat to maintain balance, preserve the position of the trunk and marginally improve leverage. The height of the heel must not exceed 4 cm ($1\frac{9}{16}$ in) nor must it extend laterally.

During training it is important to keep very warm and so a track suit should be worn. The use of a lifting belt is advised to support the trunk. Bandages are unnecessary for repetition training with light- to medium-intensity weights, unless they are used to protect an injury. During heavy training and in competition, bandages provide both physical and psychological support. Knee bandages must not exceed 8 cm ($3\frac{1}{8}$ in) in width and 2 m (6 ft 6 in) in length. Alternatively, an elastic knee cap may be worn with a maximum width of 20 cm ($7\frac{7}{8}$ in). In addition, the I.P.F. technical rules state that the belt shall not exceed 13 mm ($\frac{1}{2}$ in) in thickness and that it shall have no additional padding, bracing or supports, either on the inside or the outside.

Like any other lift, intense concentration is needed. This can be helped if at least two catchers, or spotters, are used. Such training partners can be reassuring if a heavy attempt is impending. Also, they can provide motivation and encouragement.

Because the back is vulnerable in the Squat, it is advisable to warm up thoroughly. The latter part of the warm-up should consist of several sets of back exercises, which are performed prior to squatting.

Assistance Exercises

In addition to the Squat, one or two auxiliary exercises may be performed during each workout. The following are the chief assistance exercises.

a. Prone Hyperextension This important lower back exercise is described in Chapter 5.

b. 'Good Morning' Exercise This is another standard back exercise which is also described in Chapter 5.

c. Leg Presses Inhale as the effort is made, exhale when lowering. Perform 5 sets of 5 repetitions.

d. Half Squats These are performed in the same way as the orthodox Squat, but with the bar moving through half the usual distance and the tops of thighs at an angle of about 45 degrees to the floor. Very heavy weights can be handled, thereby giving confidence. Perform 5 sets with low repetitions. For safety use stand-ins or the power rack.

e. Quarter Squats These are similar to half Squats, apart from a smaller range of movement, and the tops of the thighs at an angle of 67½ degrees to the floor. They give a tremendous psychological boost. Perform 5 sets of 3–5 repetitions. For safety use catchers or the power rack.

f. Hack Lifts (Hack Squats) These appear like a Dead Lift with the bar held behind the legs. However, they are effective in developing leg strength, especially above the knees. Inhale on the way up; exhale on the way down. Perform 5 sets of 3–5 repetitions.

g. Isometric Squats The lifter selects three or four positions in a difficult area of the Squat. The adjustable bar in the rack is set in turn to correspond to these positions. The lifter assumes his squatting position under the immovable bar. He then exerts maximum force against it for one second. After a two-minute rest pause, the movement is repeated at the next position and so on.

Training Methods

To Squat with heavy weights requires specialization. Because very heavy weights are handled, variety in training by way of exercises and weights used is advised to avoid boredom or staleness. Top powerlifters aim to be in peak form for their most important competition.

A Beginner's Schedule

The following is a suitable schedule for weight-trainers who wish to improve their Squat. This is based on a top Squat of 100 kg (220 lb).

Warm-up (Squat): 2 × 10—50 kg (110 lb)
Squat: 1 × 5—70 kg (154¼ lb); 1 × 4—77·5 kg (170¾ lb); 1 × 3—82·5 kg (181¾ lb); 1 × 2—87·5 kg (192¾ lb); 3 × 1—92·5 kg (203 lb)

Once a fortnight try to increase the intensity for singles by 5 kg (11 lb). If these go comfortably, then the weight on the bar for the whole routine can be increased by this amount. This Squat schedule forms part of an overall schedule, which should include at least one assistance exercise, such as one of those already described. It should be followed three times a week. Every two months or so the lifter should have a week's light training, followed by a change of schedule.

Ten Powerlifting: Bench Press

The Bench Press is a test of strength of the triceps muscles of the upper arms, the pectoralis major muscles of the chest and the anterior deltoid muscles of the shoulders. This lift builds great strength in these regions. Some of the world's best bench pressers have exceeded weights in excess of two and a half times their own bodyweight.

In this lift it is an advantage to have short arms. This provides shorter weight arms, especially if the insertions of the tendons of the pectoralis major and anterior deltoid muscles are not close to the shoulder joint. Moreover, short arms mean that the weight has less distance to travel. Those with long arms are at a disadvantage, but they can compensate to some extent for unfavourable leverage by building up strength through assistance exercises.

International Rules

The I.P.F. rules state:

1. The lifter may elect to assume one of the following two positions on the bench, which must be maintained during the lift:
   a. With head, trunk and legs extended on the bench, knees locked, heels on a second bench.
   b. With head, trunk (including buttocks) extended on the bench, feet flat on the floor.
2. The referee's signal shall be given when the bar is absolutely motionless at the chest.
3. After the referee's signal, the bar is pressed vertically to straight arm's length and held motionless for the referee's signal to replace the bar.
4. The lifter may use any method to bring the bar to the chest preparatory to the uplifting movement.
5. The width of the bench shall be not less than 25 cm ($9\frac{27}{32}$ in) nor more than 30 cm ($11\frac{51}{64}$ in). The bench shall be flat and level, not less than 122 cm ($48\frac{1}{32}$ in) long and the height shall be not more than 45 cm ($17\frac{5}{16}$ in) nor less than 35 cm ($13\frac{25}{32}$ in).
6. If the lifter's trunks and the bench top are not of a sufficient colour contrast to enable the officials to detect a possible raising of the buttocks, the bench top shall be covered accordingly.
7. The spacing of the hands shall not exceed 81 cm ($31\frac{7}{8}$ in) measured between the forefingers.

8. In this lift, the judges and referees shall station themselves at the best points of vantage.
9. For those lifters who elect to use the second position and whose feet do not touch the floor, the platform may be built up to provide firm footing.
10. A maximum of four and minimum of two spotter-loaders shall be mandatory. However, the lifter may enlist one or more of the official spotter-loaders to assist him in removing the bar from the racks.

Causes for Disqualification

a. During the uplifting, any change of the elected lifting position.
b. Any raising or shifting of the lifter's head, shoulders, buttocks, or legs from the bench, or movement of the feet.
c. Any heaving or bouncing of the bar from the chest.
d. Allowing the bar to sink excessively into the lifter's chest prior to the uplift.
e. Any uneven extension of the arms.
f. Stopping of the bar during the Press proper.
g. Any touching of the bar by the spotters before the referee's signal to replace the bar.
h. Failure to wait for the referee's signal.
i. Touching against the uprights of the bench with the feet.
j. Touching against the uprights of the bench with the shoulders.
k. Allowing the bar to touch the uprights of the bench during the uplifting.

Technique of the Bench Press

Preparation

a. The lifter ensures that the bar is safely resting on the stands with the bench directly in the front of the middle of the bar and at right angles to the bar.
b. The lifter sits on one end of the bench with his feet flat on the floor. Usually the feet are turned out, with the heels about hip width apart. Slight adjustments should be made to achieve the most comfortable, firm and stable position. Most lifters aim to have vertical shins. Shorter lifters may need to raise their heels by placing blocks of wood between their feet and the platform.
c. The lifter lies on the bench with his head, shoulders and buttocks touching the top of the bench. These must be kept in contact with the bench throughout the lift. Also, the feet must be kept motionless and in contact with the platform throughout the lift. It is important that the platform is not too smooth; otherwise the feet may slide.

d. The head and shoulders are pushed towards the buttocks to form an arch of the back. This raises the rib-cage, thereby shortening the distance the bar has to travel. The whole of the body is braced throughout the lift, while the feet exert downward pressure on the platform.

   N.B. In the alternative version of this lift, the head, trunk and legs are allowed to be in contact with the bench. The knees must be kept locked. This version is not recommended because it makes it difficult to arch the back adequately. Moreover, there is a tendency to slide along the bench and the exertion of downward pressure by the legs is difficult. However, certain lifters such as paraplegics have to use this style (see Chapter 14). The alternative version is shown in Figure 10.

e. The lifter grasps the bar firmly with the widest and most comfortable grip—the limit is 81 cm ($31\frac{7}{8}$ in) measured between the forefingers.

f. The loaders, sometimes known as 'spotters' or 'catchers', hand the bar to the lifter, who receives it at arms' length. He receives the bar over the joints of his shoulders. From that position he lowers the bar to the chest where it is held motionless and ready for the referee's signal to start the Press proper.

The Pressing Movement

a. The lowering of the bar to the chest must be controlled. The prime movers (anterior deltoids, pectoralis major and triceps muscles) stretch in this process, with a slowing up of the bar as it arrives at the lower part of the pectoral muscles of the chest. The elbows rotate inward to the sides of the chest in order to act as efficiently as possible. As the bar is lowered, a deep inhalation is taken so as to keep the chest firm and raised.

b. At the referee's signal to press, the feet press firmly into the platform and the arms drive the bar along an upward and slightly backward line of action, aiming to finish the Press with the bar over the shoulder joints. The elbows are eased outward during this movement. Pressing back too soon can cause the bar's gravity line to fall over the neck too early. Consequently the weight arms of the humerus bones are at a mechanical disadvantage. Aim to ease the bar backward and upward in a straight line.

c. The bar must not stop during the Press. If the bar slows down, it is recommended that short, quick breaths are taken. The lifter must not hold his breath, and he should exhale just before the Press is finished.

d. At the 'sticking point' or disadvantageous area, the lifter must

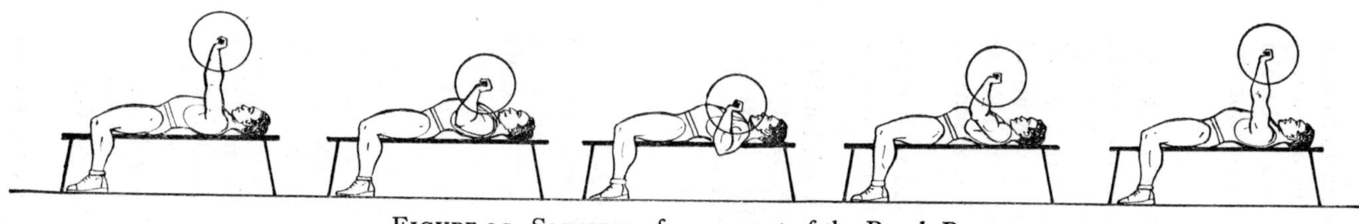

FIGURE 9*a*. Sequence of movement of the Bench Press

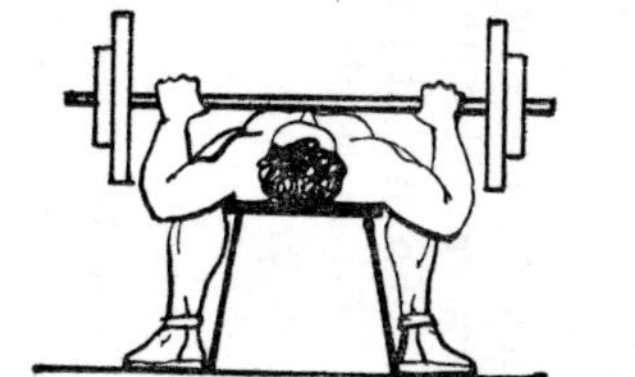

FIGURE 9*b*. End view of the Bench Press

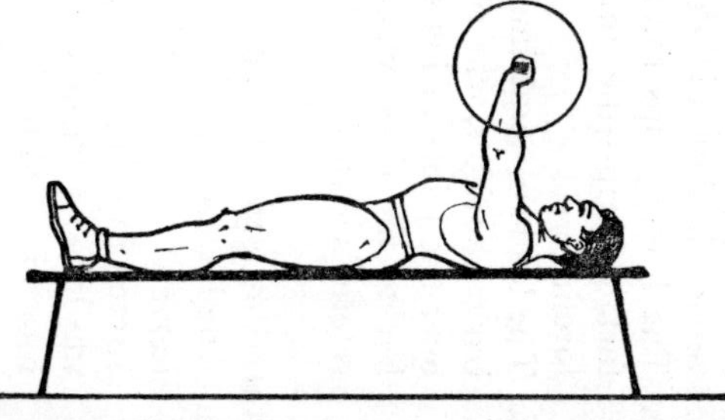

FIGURE 10. Alternative version of the Bench Press

continue to press the bar upward. At the same time the feet, hips, shoulders and head resist with downward pressure.

e. The elbows must be straight with the bar held motionless at the conclusion of the lift. The lifter must avoid touching the stands with the bar or his arms or shoulders.

Remarks

The preceding technique is a safe, standard technique. Individuals may vary parts of it to suit their own physical make-up. However, a vast departure from this method is not advocated. It is better to spend a little time to master a good, mechanically and physiologically sound method. This may mean dropping to lighter weights and performing more repetitions. But the long-term benefits will be worthwhile.

Short arms and a deep thorax are an advantage for a bench presser. But great strength in the triceps, deltoids and pectoral muscles is essential for top performances. Suitable training on the lift plus assistance exercises can help to improve strength.

Assistance Exercises

If needed, one or two of the following exercises may be chosen for incorporation into the main training schedule:

1. Barbell Bench Press Variations So as to provide variety and to place the work on different areas of the muscles involved, one of the following movements may be selected. The mode of performance is similar to the Bench Press already described.

a. Barbell Bench Press. Use a wide, medium or narrow grip for 5 sets of 3–5 repetitions.
b. Inclined Bench Press. As for (a).
c. Declined Bench Press. As for (a).

2. Dumb-bell Bench Press Variations These can be performed on a flat, inclined or declined bench with the bells parallel to the body, turned outward or at right angles to the body. Use either pyramid progression or 5 sets of 3–5 repetitions.

3. Cheating Bench Press The preparation for this movement is similar to the competition Bench Press. The pressing part, however, is assisted by a vigorous, upward thrust of the hips, enabling heavier weights to be used. This gives confidence and the feel of heavy weights. Usually 5 sets of 1–3 repetitions are used.

CAUTION: spotters should be at hand to take the weight if the lifter is in difficulty.

4. Supporting Exercise, Lying on Bench This movement assists in developing strength in the final lockout. With the stands set so that the bar can be grasped over the shoulders and with elbows slightly bent, lock out the arms and hold for one second. This movement enables very heavy weights to be used. It is useful in the last few weeks before a competition. Perform 5 sets of 1–2 repetitions.

5. *Dumb-bells' Lateral Raise, Lying* This exercise is used for pectoralis strengthening. The bells are carefully lowered on straight arms with a sideways movement, in line with the shoulders. They are then raised upward to a finishing position over the shoulders. Heavier weights can be handled by using a bent arm version, which shortens the weight arm. Perform 3 or 4 sets of 5–8 repetitions.

6. *Pullover and Press on Bench* This exercise is mainly for the triceps. It is performed using a narrow grip with palms uppermost. While lying comfortably on the bench, ensure feet and legs are firmly anchored by tucking them under a barbell or getting a partner to sit across the lifter's thighs. From the chest lower the bar in a circular motion over the head until it is some 30 cm (12 in) below the head. Keeping the elbows bent, pull the bar back to the chest, then press it to arm's length. Lower to the chest and repeat for 5 sets of 3–5 repetitions. Use two complete breaths to each exercise cycle.

7. *Parallel Bar Dips* This exercise is to develop great triceps strength. With weights fastened to the lifter's belt dip from a straight arms' position on the parallel bars to an arms fully bent position. Then press up to straight arms. Breathe in on the way down and out on the way up. Perform 5 sets of 5 repetitions.

8. *Elbow (Triceps) Extensions* These may be performed with a barbell when seated or standing. Dumb-bells or swingbells may be used also. Using a narrow grip, extend the elbows against resistance from a fully bent position. An effective variation is to press down on the bar of a wall pulley exerciser ('lat' machine). Inhale on the effort; exhale on lowering. Perform 4 sets of 6 repetitions.

Training Methods

There are many effective training methods for the Bench Press. They are included in overall powerlifting schedules, varying according to whether the lifter is just starting to train seriously or whether he is an experienced lifter with competitions in mind.

A Beginner's Schedule

This is based on a top Bench Press of 67·5 kg (148¾ lb)

Warm-up: Bench Press 2 × 10—35 kg (77 lb)
Bench Press: 1 × 5—45 kg (99 lb); 1 × 4—50 kg (110 lb); 1 × 3—55 kg (121¼ lb); 1 × 2—60 kg (132¼ lb); 3 × 1—65 kg (143¼ lb)

Once a fortnight try to increase the weight used for singles. If these improve comfortably by at least 2·5 kg (5¼ lb), increase the weight on the bar by this amount for the whole routine. If there is no improvement, perform 5 sets of 2–3 repetitions after the singles, making sure to take at least three minutes' rest between sets. Train three times weekly. Change the schedule every eight weeks or so.

Eleven Powerlifting: Dead Lift

The Dead Lift is mainly a test of strength of the erectores spinae muscles which run along the side of the vertebrae. Also, it requires tremendous strength of grip, hips, legs, shoulder girdle and upper back. Some of the world's best deadlifters have succeeded with lifts in excess of four times their bodyweight.

Two styles of Dead Lift are used. The one advocated here uses a flat back, which is a safe technique. Another method employs a rounded spine, which is not recommended generally because it may be conducive to injuries of the spine. Any risk of lower back strains, or sprains of ligaments, or damage to the intervertebral discs is to be avoided at all costs.

Long arms may not help the Bench Press, but they are an advantage in dead lifting.

International Rules

The I.P.F. rules state:

1. The bar must be laid horizontally in front of the lifter's feet, gripped with an optional grip with both hands, and uplifted with one continuous motion until the lifter is standing erect. At the completion of the lift, the knees must be locked and the shoulders thrust back. The referee's signal shall indicate the time when the bar is held motionless in the final position, or in any stopped position.

Causes for Disqualification

a. Any stopping of the bar before it reaches the final position.
b. Failure to stand erect.
c. Failure to lock the knees.
d. Supporting the bar on the thighs.
e. Lowering the bar before the referee's signal to replace the bar on the platform.
f. Any raising of the bar, or any deliberate attempt to do so, from the platform shall count as an attempt.
g. Any shifting of the feet during performance of the lift.
h. Any raising of the toes or heels.
i. Allowing the bar to return to the platform without maintaining control with both hands.

Technique of the Dead Lift

PREPARATION

a. Assume the 'get set' position with the back flat and as upright as possible. The head is kept high.
b. Reverse the grip to prevent the bar turning, preferably using a 'hook' technique with the first two fingers wrapped round the thumb as well as the bar.
c. The handspacing should be a little wider than shoulder width, measured between the index fingers. The arms are kept straight. Very wide handspacing with one shoulder externally rotated involves the risk of injury.
d. The feet should be approximately hip width apart. The toes may be turned out slightly. Heels on the lifter's boots are unnecessary.

THE LIFTING MOVEMENT

a. The actual Dead Lift should be a gradual lift from the platform, using leg, hip and back strength.
b. Gently ease the bar into the shins, keeping the back as upright as possible. Try to increase the angle formed by the shins and thighs at the knee-joints. Those with long shin bones have to get their hips up relatively quickly, but not too fast.
c. Push the feet firmly into the platform, while looking ahead and keeping the chin tucked in to prevent the posterior spinal ligaments from slackening.
d. The hips must not rotate and must be kept level throughout the movement. Avoid rounding the spine to prevent injury. The bar must be kept moving.
e. Use the shoulder girdle retractor and upper back muscles to brace the shoulders back before the conclusion of the lift. Knees and hips must be extended. Do not relax the grip.
f. It is advisable to breathe in before starting the lift off the platform. Gradually exhale on rising.

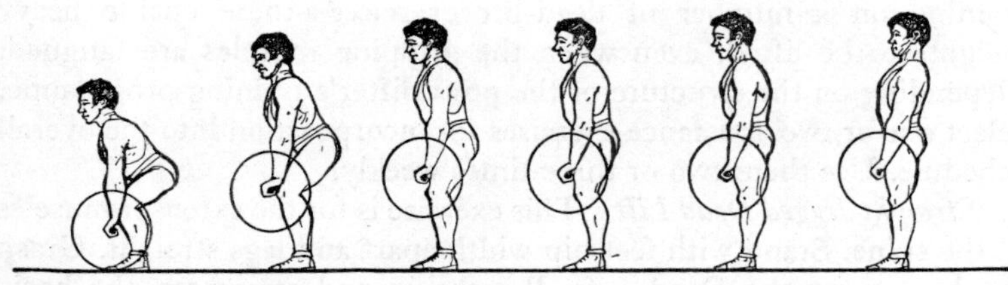

FIGURE 11. Sequence of movement of the Dead Lift

LOWERING THE WEIGHT

a Lower the bar under control to the platform. Fight hard to maintain a strong grip.

b. A sudden release of the bar may catch the muscles 'off guard', with possible injury.

Remarks

The preceding technique is safe. Although a few top-line lifters use a rounded-back style, do not be tempted to imitate them because of the risk of injury.

If you are changing from the rounded-back style to the safer flat-back style, which is more efficient mechanically and anatomically, drop your training poundages for a few weeks, or months, if necessary. Perform sufficient repetitions in the early stages to eliminate faulty habits. Then build up gradually to heavier weights with the flat-back style. If the old technique is not extinguished, then repeat the process of going back to the beginning with lighter weights, remembering to use the legs and keeping the back flat.

It is advisable to use a lifting belt to give support to the whole of the trunk. The use of powdered resin on the palms, fingers and thumbs assists the grip. Also, wear a tracksuit in training in order to keep warm. Do not discard too much clothing in the gymnasium since local chilling can occur.

Some deadlifters lubricate their thighs to reduce the effects of friction between the barbell and their quadricep muscles. The use of oil, grease or other lubricant is strictly forbidden by the I.P.F. However, powder such as talcum or magnesium carbonate is an acceptable substitute.

Assistance Exercises

The squatting part of the programme builds up leg and hip strength. Assistance exercises for the Dead Lift are, as a rule, for strengthening the back, the trapezius muscles of the upper back and the grip. The following exercises are used by power-lifters and dead-lift specialists. Occasionally wrist straps, which wrap around the bar, are used in training on a number of dead-lift exercises—these enable heavy weights to be lifted, even when the gripping muscles are fatigued. Depending on the structure of the powerlifter's training programme, select one or two assistance exercises for incorporation into the overall schedule. Use them two or three times weekly.

1. Straight-legged Dead Lift This exercise is for the extensor muscles of the spine. Stand with feet hip width apart and legs straight. Grasp the bar as for the Dead Lift. Breathe in and straighten the back. Exhale at or just before the finish. Avoid using a rounded spine—keep the back flat. Perform 5 sets of 3–5 repetitions. Sometimes this movement is performed while the lifter stands on blocks or a bench. This enables him to use a greater range of movement. He should not use very heavy weights in this movement.

2. *Dead Lift off Blocks* This assistance movement is for developing the upper part of the lift. The weight is lifted off blocks from about knee height. The technique is similar to the Dead Lift, only the back is more upright at the start. Perform 3 sets of 8 repetitions or alternatively 5 sets of 5 repetitions. Sometimes the weights are increased for repetitions of threes, twos and singles.

3. *Dead Lift Supports* This exercise is for control, the back and the grip. Assistants lift the weight to the upright position, where it is held for at least one second. Use up to 10 per cent more than the best Dead Lift. Perform 5 singles.

4. *Prone Hyperextension* This is described on page 57. Perform 3 sets of 10 repetitions.

5. *'Good Morning' Exercise* This is described on page 57. Perform 3 sets of 8 repetitions.

6. *Bent-over Rowing* This is described on page 58. Perform 3 sets of 8 repetitions.

7. *Shoulder Shrug* This is described on page 59. Perform 4 sets of 6 repetitions.

8. *Grip Exercises* These have been described in Chapter 5.

9. *Reverse Curl* This exercise is for the gripping and forearm muscles. Stand up with a light barbell with hands spaced shoulder width apart and knuckles facing the front. From a starting position with arms straight, bend the elbows until the bar touches the neck. Lower and repeat. Breathe in on the effort and out as the bar is lowered. Perform 3 sets of 8 repetitions.

Training Methods

Refer to the sections on training methods for the Squat (pages 97–98). Training for the Dead Lift involves similar principles. However, because more areas of the body are involved, the Dead Lift can be more demanding on the lifter. For this reason, most powerlifters deadlift only twice a week. Also they attempt heavy Dead Lifts once every two or three weeks. A heavy workout should be followed by a lighter one. Sometimes a heavy week's work is followed by a light week's work for recovery reasons.

A Beginner's Schedule

Since beginners use lighter weights than seasoned powerlifters, they may train on the Dead Lift three times weekly. They can base their deadlifting schedule on the routine suggested for the Squat on page 98.

Twelve Powerlifting: Advanced Training Methods

The serious powerlifter trains for competitions in order to win titles or matches. Some train to break records on individual power lifts. This requires advanced training of a strenuous nature. When training for a best total, sometimes it is necessary to specialize on a particularly weak lift in order to raise the level of the over-all total. But this should not be done at the expense of reduced performance on the other lifts. The powerlifter's aims and objectives must be clearly defined. His main aim may be to win a particular championship on a certain date. This means he has to plan according to the calendar with realistic targets in mind for each of the lifts. A simple training cycle is advised, which consists of a preparatory period of several months, followed by a competitive period of four to six weeks.

Specific objectives have to be taken into account; for example, a relatively poor Bench Press may have to be brought up to a better standard or the powerlifter may have a technical problem to solve. Individual circumstances have to be taken into account when devising advanced training programmes. Therefore, some guidance will be given in planning the training for each lift as well as composite schedules and other elements of advanced training.

For much of the year many prominent powerlifters use a standard schedule which can be varied. Maximum lifts are used sporadically. After a few weeks of general conditioning with and without weights the idea is to train progressively for strength—with light-, medium- and heavy-intensity weights up to some four or six weeks before the competition. Also, the volume of the training load is varied. At this point, assistance exercises are reduced in number while training on the remaining movements becomes more arduous right up to seven or ten days before the big event. Then the lifter tapers off, cutting out non-essential exercises and any extraneous activity at work and at home. This should leave him with peak strength and energy for the competition. For the last three or four days before the competition a complete rest is taken from training. On the day of the competition itself, as much rest as possible is taken. After the competition, at least a week's rest is taken, before beginning light training prior to starting a new training cycle.

Advanced Schedules for the Squat

The following standard schedule is for use in the first part of the strength build-up. It can be incorporated into the over-all workout. It should be used three times weekly.

Warm-up (free Squats): 1 × 25
Prone hyperextension: 3 × 10
Front Squat: 2 × 8; 2 × 6
Squat: 1 × 5; 1 × 4; 1 × 3; 3 × 1—intensity progressively increasing during 'heavy' sessions up to 90–95 per cent of max. Try limits monthly
Half or quarter Squat: 5 × 3
Other power lifts: to suit individual requirements

The full workout, depending on the length of rest pauses between sets (one and a half to three minutes), lasts for two to two and a half hours. The schedule should be changed every eight weeks if there is evidence of staleness or lack of progress. The temptation to use maximum weights every workout should be avoided at all costs since this can lead to overtraining. Aim to increase weights every fortnight.

Here is another advanced squatting schedule suitable for use in the first part of the strength build-up.

Warm-up (Squats without bar): 1 × 15–25
other free exercises: 1 × 15–25
Squat: 1 × 10—60 per cent of max.; 1 × 10—70 per cent of max.; 6 × 6—increase intensity each set to fifth set, where 90 per cent of max. can be used once a week. Drop the intensity by 10 per cent on the sixth set
Half Squat or hack lift: 5 × 3
Other power lifts: to suit individual requirements

After six to eight weeks the second part of the strength build-up starts. The squatting section of the schedule is then changed to more sets of lower repetitions with heavier weights. This is an increase in the volume of the training load and barbell intensity. The following is a typical method of applying the increase to the Squat.

Monday (heavy): 1 × 8; 1 × 6; 5 × 3; 3 × 2; 3 × 1—up to 95 per cent of max.
Wednesday (light): 1 × 8; 1 × 6; 3 × 5—up to 70 per cent of max.
Friday (medium): 1 × 8; 1 × 6; 1 × 4; 3 × 3—up to 80 per cent of max.

In general maximum weights should be used only every three or four weeks to measure progress. Heavy training sessions are followed by lighter workouts for recuperation purposes. This is brought about by decreasing the training load and the intensity so that the number of repetitions and the weight on the bar are decreased by approximately 20 per cent of the heavy load and intensity.

Advanced Schedules for the Bench Press

As with the Squat, advanced powerlifters tend to use a standard training programme which is progressive and flexible. Some general preparation is made using light weights and several exercises. This is followed by a strengthening phase with progressive increases in training load and barbell intensity. Then four weeks before a competition the weight is increased right up to ten days before the event, when the lifter tapers off, entirely cutting out assistance exercises.

The following standard schedule may be used in the strength build-up. It should be performed three times a week, and should be incorporated into the overall workout.

Warm-up (Bench Press): 1–2 × 10
Bench Press: 2 × 5; 2 × 3; 2 × 2; 3 × 1—up to 90–95 per cent of best lift on 'heavy' workouts
Bench Press with dumb-bells: 5 × 5; change to 5 × 3 on 'heavy' workouts
Parallel bar dips: 5 × 5

The schedule may be used to suit individual circumstances. Limits should be tried every three or four weeks to measure progress. Increases can then be made in the actual bench pressing section of the training schedule. The work must be kept in proportion to the remainder of the rest of the training schedule. Cut back or change the routine if undue fatigue or staleness appears. However, near a competition change to heavier weights with sets of lower repetitions and singles as with the Squat.

Some powerlifters favour 5 sets of 5 repetitions as a basic strengthening schedule. This helps to increase muscle bulk as well as basic strength. Increases in weight, in sets of threes, twos and singles are made near competitions. The arrangement of these depends on the individual lifter, as well as the remainder of his training schedule.

Advanced Schedules for the Dead Lift

Most advanced powerlifters do not train on the Dead Lift every workout, even when training only three times weekly. Squatting, together with various leg and lighter back-strengthening exercises, all contribute to the strength required for deadlifting. As a general rule, deadlifting should be practised twice a week, with limit attempts every sixth workout or less frequently.

Many powerlifters use a basic strengthening schedule for deadlifting of 5 sets of 5 repetitions, progressing after several weeks to a more intense schedule employing sets of threes, twos and singles with increasing weights. Heavy weights must be used for competition preparation.

Composite Schedules for Powerlifters

Although a number of lifters have been known to train five or even six times weekly, this cannot be kept up for any great length of time by most powerlifters. Many train three times weekly, blending into their programme the Squat, Press on Bench, Dead Lift and assistance exercises.

Because individual circumstances vary, there are many examples of composite training schedules for advanced powerlifters. Coaches and lifters have to arrange training plans according to experience, the lifter's deficiencies and capacity, training time available, the date of the next major tournament, mental and physical problems and other factors. A detailed record of training, kept in diary form, will enable effective training (or otherwise) to be pinpointed. It should contain details of training load and barbell intensity, and the phases decided upon for general conditioning, strengthening and competition preparation.

To avoid boredom, or sometimes staleness, variation of the training programme is necessary. This can be arranged in several ways, but there are two popular training structures, one of which uses different schedules on alternate workouts or weeks, and the other a change of sets, repetitions, and weight in training on the major power lifts, plus a variation in assistance exercises. In either case the lifter aims at progressive increases in training intensity over several months, culminating in top performance on the day of the competition.

The following is an example of an alternate training schedule method for building up strength. It was used successfully by the 1973 World 56 kg powerlifting champion, Precious McKenzie, M.B.E.

Weeks 1 and 3 (heavy)	*Weeks 2 and 4 (medium)*
Monday	
Squat: 5 × 3; 1 × 5	Incline Bench Press: 5 × 3
Bench Press: 5 × 3; 1 × 5	Shoulder shrugs: 5 × 3
Dead Lift: 5 × 3; 1 × 5	Half Squat: 5 × 3
	Upright rowing: 5 × 3
Wednesday	
Front Squat: 5 × 3; 1 × 5	Decline Bench Press: 5 × 3
Dumb-bell Bench Press: 5 × 3	Front Squat: 5 × 3
Dead Lift off blocks: 5 × 3	Abdominal raise: 5 × max. reps.
Friday	
Hack Lift: 5 × 3	Bench Press (wide grip); 3 × 3

Half Squat: 5 × 3	Half Squat: 5 × 3
Leg press: 5 × 3	Bent-over rowing: 5 × 3

This alternate training schedule may be followed for a three-month period. Limits may be tried every month, provided no major contest is imminent.

Here is another example of an alternative training schedule, based on heavy and medium strengthening schedules, each used on alternate days.

Heavy schedule	*Medium schedule*
Prone hyperextension: 3 × 10	'Good morning' exercise: 3 × 8
Squat: 1 × 5; 3 × 3; 2 × 2; 3 × 1	Squat: 1 × 5; 5 × 3
Bench Press: 1 × 5; 4 × 3; 2 × 2; 3 × 1	Bench Press: 1 × 5; 5 × 3
Dead Lift: 2 × 5; 4 × 3; 1 × 2; 3 × 1	Dead Lift: 2 × 6; 4 × 3
Abdominal raise: 3 × 12	Reverse curl: 3 × 8
Mobility exercises: 5 minutes	Running: 5–10 minutes

The following is an example of a normal schedule to be used three times weekly. It may be varied to suit individual preferences.

Warm-up: free Squats, free back extensions, press-ups

'Good morning' exercise:	3 × 8
or	
Straight-legged Dead Lift:	3 × 8
Squat:	5 × 5
Bench Press:	4 × 5; 3 × 2
Dead Lift	4 × 6
or	
Shoulder shrug:	4 × 6
Inclined situp:	3 × 10
Running:	5 minutes, including rest pauses

Two weeks before a competition, discard assistance exercises and step up the weights for the three lifts.

Warm-up:	Squats 2 × 12; floor dips 1 × 12
Squat:	2 × 5; 2 × 3; 3 × 2; 3 × 1
Bench Press:	2 × 3; 3 × 2; 3 × 1
Dead Lift:	1 × 5; 5 × 2; 3 × 1

Competition Preparation

Ten days before the competition or record attempt, assistance exercises are eliminated to conserve energy. Usually a three-day rest is taken before the competition or record attempt, with as much rest as possible on the day of the event.

The warm-up should start about thirty minutes before the lifters are due on the platform, starting with a few free exercises to stimulate the circulation generally. Exercises such as free Squats, press-ups, arm circling and sidebends may be used for the first five minutes of the warm-up. Then use prone hyperextensions, followed by the 'good morning' exercise, 3 sets × 10 repetitions with light weights to prepare the back muscles for the heavy attempts to follow. Then proceed warming up with the barbell itself—this should be similar to the one to be used in the competition. Start with five light repetitions, followed by progressive increases in the barbell's intensity, using decreasing repetitions of fours, threes, twos and singles on each lift. The singles may go as high as 95 per cent of the suggested starting poundages, which should be realistic and determined by experience.

A positive mental attitude towards the competition is very important. Previous successful training and competition gives confidence. On the day of the event as well as the day before, diet should be predominantly of carbohydrates for energy purposes. If there are bodyweight problems, then the food and fluid intake has to be regulated with care.

After a major contest, at least a week's layoff is advised. This can be followed by up to a month's 'active rest' on other physical activities such as non-contact sports and fitness training. Then light training with weights may be resumed prior to starting up a complete training cycle for the next big competition. In most cases a 10 per cent increase in tonnage is planned for the following year.

Thirteen Teaching Weightlifting

Reasons for Teaching Weightlifting

Although many teachers are happy to include weightlifting in their physical education programmes in schools, youth clubs, evening classes and colleges, some regard the area as controversial. Therefore, the following reasons are given to justify its inclusion in the physical education programme for boys.

1. It is one area in a wide sphere of physical activities which includes back management techniques.
2. Balanced strength and development is acquired in an enjoyable way. Increases in these basic features have been shown to improve self-confidence and self-image.
3. Increased strength and muscular development is a precaution against injury in other sports.
4. The classical lifts are aesthetic, skilled movements. The learning of the weightlifting skill contributes to education.
5. Training intensity, standards for recognized awards, or competition performance, are related to the bodyweight of the boy. In many other sports the smaller boy has to compete on unequal terms.
6. Weight-training and lifting can have a definite carry-over value to other activities.
7. Carefully graded training can contribute towards good health. Apart from the increased strength of anti-gravity muscles which tend to counteract malposture, bone growth is stimulated in adolescents, particularly the compact layer and spongy substances.
8. The set system employs an alternation of activity followed by relaxation which not only benefits the pupil physically, but can also be effective in reducing emotional tension.
9. Regular, tangible improvements are rewarding and bring about feelings of self-satisfaction, an important quality for under-achievers. Each step of progress is part of a continual challenge to achieve.
10. Exercises with weights can contribute to the development of organic vigour, an important objective in physical education.
11. Weightlifting entails athletic qualities valued by physical educators.
12. Unlike the majority of body-contact sports, weightlifting is practically injury free.

13. With the introduction of various levels of schoolboy weightlifting championships in recent years, the teaching of competitive weightlifting may start a boy on a sporting career.
14. Since some boys are dissatisfied with the traditional activities in their physical education programmes, exercises with weights may prove to be acceptable to them.
15. Certain categories of disabled youths can practise suitable weightlifting movements when other sports are debarred.
16. Weight-training or lifting over a period of time demands the application of discipline and persistence. In these days of 'drop-outs' such qualities are worthy of pursuit.
17. Weightlifting can be fun and have a lasting enjoyment for its own sake.

Teaching Weightlifting in Schools and Colleges

In many schools weight-training or lifting is organized on an extra-curricular basis. Usually this is in the form of a club which meets after school, catering for small numbers only. Some schools operate option schemes which offer a choice of a variety of activities to boys in the upper school. Weightlifting has a place here and it is within the curriculum.

However, class teaching in the physical education lesson is an economic way of dispensing the necessary knowledge as it caters for relatively large numbers. Moreover, it is a convenient time to deal with general faults.

Equipment

Existing equipment such as barbells and dumb-bells used for circuit training, physical education benches, and sticks and mats for protecting the floor, may be used for small groups. If this equipment is supplemented, eventually weight-training can be introduced as a class activity. There is a place for using improvised disc weights made of wood and fitted with conventional or home-made collars to bars of tubular steel. The advantages are lightness, cheapness, and that the diameter of the discs can be full size, yet weigh only 2·5 kg ($5\frac{1}{2}$ lb). In contrast to small standard discs of that weight, this permits flat-back techniques to be taught, even to long-limbed boys.

For class teaching there should be a bar, collars and weights for every five boys at the most. One barbell set for every three boys is better. Thus a class of thirty boys require a minimum of six barbells, although ten barbells are preferable.

Organization

The gymnasium layout for class teaching is straightforward. The teacher organizes units of equipment and groups of boys of about the same strength. Groups are well spaced out for safety. The teacher stands where he is easily seen and heard by the boys and where he can see them. Typical configurations of groups are: along three sides of a rectangle or trapezium; in a semi-circle; or just spaced out freely in front of the teacher. There should be no remote groups in corners of the gymnasium or in the storeroom.

Equipment is set out at the beginning of the lesson. Bars, weights, benches, box tops and mats should be placed in orderly fashion and safety factors checked. The boys may have to practise this procedure several times before it is regarded as safe and efficient. Command-response methods may be used at first in order to make this aspect of organization slick and smooth. Also, discipline can be established in this way; later, teacher-imposed control is replaced by inner discipline from the boys themselves. The training of boys in the drills of collecting, carrying and the setting out of equipment may take time, but it is worthwhile.

Standing in

Correct methods of standing in have to be taught in the early stages. For Squats and overhead movements, two boys act as 'spotters' or stand ins, one at each end of the barbell. They should be alert, standing with feet apart and following the end of the barbell with both of their hands underneath the bar with palms uppermost. Their job is to prevent the bar from falling on to the performer. They will grasp and support the bar at each end if it is clear that the performer cannot complete the movement. A verbal signal such as 'take it' helps this manoeuvre.

For the Bench Press and similar movements lying down, two boys lift the barbell from the floor or stands, using a flat-back technique. Both hands grip the end of the bar in a stirrup fashion, palms uppermost, and with one hand placed beneath the other. The performer takes his grasp of the barbell: when ready he tells the stand ins, who release it. Upon completion of the exercise, or in the event of an incomplete movement, the stand ins take the bar carefully and replace it on the floor or stands.

Lesson Plans

A Weight-training Lesson for Beginners

The following structure is typical of a forty-minute weight-training lesson for beginners.

a. Introductory Part (*ten minutes*)

i. Running and free exercises for all the major muscle groups.

ii. Partner activities of a strengthening nature (medicine balls may be used).
iii. Skip-jumping variations.
iv. Related warm-up activities with elements in common with the weight-training exercises to follow (for example, Squats, press-ups, trunk heaves on low beams, handstand against a partner and so on; staves may be used for practising shadow movements).

b. Main Part (twenty-five minutes)
In this section a schedule of exercises for beginners is taught (see page 45). Always keep to the correct physiological sequence.
i. Arm exercise.
ii. Shoulder exercise.
iii. Leg exercise.
iv. Chest exercise.
v. Back exercise.
vi. Exercises for other regions (for example, calves or abdominals).

c. Concluding Part (five minutes)
Game such as volleyball, basketball or relays.

Lessons for Intermediate Pupils

Lessons for those beyond the beginners' stage take longer since the schedule usually contains more difficult exercises. Also, the rest pauses are longer. Intermediate and advanced pupils are taught weight-training or lifting on a club basis. In the upper school the weightlifting club is extra-curricular and complementary to the main physical education.

Lessons are divided into three parts.

a. Introductory Part (ten to fifteen minutes)
This consists of a thorough warm-up, composed of general and specific movements. Flexibility exercises and some related practices belong to this section.

b. Main Part (duration varies according to the schedule)
The movements of the training schedule are practised here. Direct teaching and incidental coaching methods are used.

c. Concluding Part (six minutes)
This is in the form of recovery training.

First-stage Weightlifting Lessons for Beginners

Weightlifting should not be taught until a boy has practised weight-training and skills assistance exercises to at least the intermediate stage, by which time he will have built up a fair degree of strength, development and control.

The following sets out lesson plans for teaching the Snatch and the Clean and Jerk during a thirteen-week term.

a. Warm-up (ten to fifteen minutes)

The following exercises should be varied slightly for each lesson.

i. Free running, skipping and jumping exercises.

ii. Free exercises consisting of trunk bends, arm circling, side-bends, squats, lunges and handstands.

iii. Flexibility exercises for the ankles, hips, trunk and shoulders.

iv. Shadow lifting movements with staves or empty bars.

b. Main Part (duration varies according to the schedules)

This can involve more than one schedule, so the lesson content in this section may not be the same in consecutive lessons. Examples are shown in the chapters dealing with the specific lifts. Only one complex lifting movement is taught or revised in any one lesson. Light weights are used with an emphasis on technique. The split Snatch would be taught by introducing assistance exercises.

Snatch (Lessons 1–4)

i. Snatch pulls.

ii. Snatch balance exercises.

iii. Arm action with the bar only.

iv. Full movement.

When these parts are put together to form the complete Snatch, the intensity of the barbell should not exceed half the boy's bodyweight. The lift is shaped by further practice and coaching. The intensity of the barbell remains fixed until satisfactory movements are acquired. Several lessons later, flexible pupils who are natural squatters should be tested on overhead squats. If these are performed easily and under control when in a low squat position, then the squat Snatch may be introduced, using the same method as for the split Snatch.

The Clean (split version) and Jerk is taught as two movements, each of which is broken down into parts and practised sectionally. A separate lesson is allocated to each movement. The Jerk is taught first.

Jerk (Lessons 5–7)

i. Push jerks 3 × 3.

ii. Jerk balance exercise 3 × 3.

iii. Full movement 5 complete lifts.

Split Clean (Lessons 8–10)

i. Clean pulls 3 × 3.

ii. Clean receiving position (lunges) 3 × 3.

iii. Arm action with bar only 3 × 3.

iv. Full movement 5 complete lifts.

Clean and Jerk (Lessons 11–13)

The complete Clean and Jerk is practised in the skills part of the lesson. The intensity of the bar should be 60–65 per cent of the boy's bodyweight. No increases in weight should be made until a fair degree of skill is demonstrated. In the following term small increases may be made at intervals of three to four weeks.

Also in the following term, the squat Clean may be introduced to those with the necessary flexibility and balance.

c. Concluding Part (*six to ten minutes*)
Running variations at a moderate pace: forward, backward, sideways, with high knees-raising and with variations in stride length. Stretching and trunk exercises.

SECOND-STAGE WEIGHTLIFTING LESSONS FOR BEGINNERS

Warm-up: as in previous lessons.
Main part (varies according to time available):

Monday		*Wednesday*		*Friday*	
Push Jerk	3 × 3	Jerk (from rack)	5 × 2	Clean	5 × 2
Snatch	5 × 2	Power Snatch with dip	3 × 3	Snatch pulls	3 × 3
Front or lunge squats	3 × 5	Clean pulls	3 × 3	Front or squat lunge	3 × 5

Concluding part As in previous lessons. Wednesday's schedule may be substituted by a conventional physical education lesson. After a term, the number of exercises can be increased to four or five, depending on the capacity of the pupil.

Teaching Methods

CLASS-TEACHING TECHNIQUE

With this method the teacher uses a 'direct' approach because he chooses the activity. The simple movements are taught by the *gestalt* or 'whole' method. The boys learn partly by imitation and partly by responding to the teacher's suggestions. Much of the vitality of the lesson stems from the teacher, whose interest, personality and enthusiasm should be transmitted to the pupils in a businesslike manner. When introducing the basic weight-training movements of a beginner's schedule, the teacher invariably uses the following approach.

a. He explains the movement concisely.
b. He gives a precise demonstration.
c. The boys do the exercise.
d. The teacher coaches and makes positive comments.

For clarity, these four stages are considered in more detail.

a. Explanation A clear, unhurried, concise explanation of the exercise influences the learning of the class. Long-winded, irrelevant statements do not stimulate interest—rather they are likely to bore the class. What is said should be consistent with the demonstration which follows. The very formal drill-type commands used during the organization part of the lesson are replaced by natural, conversational tones. Muscle action and the names of muscles should not be mentioned, as movements not muscles are represented in the boys' higher nervous systems.

b. Demonstration The demonstration must be performed in good style. Three repetitions are sufficient to convey a mental picture to the pupils. The demonstration should be performed at a normal exercise tempo—otherwise the model to be copied will convey the wrong impression. It is the teacher's job to impart knowledge. Therefore, exact starting and finishing positions and movement patterns must be demonstrated.

c. Activity The boys learn the exercise by doing it. The boys in each group should be numbered one, two, three and so on. Those numbered one perform specified exercise repetitions, say eight, while the teacher coaches without stopping the boys. When the barbells are replaced on the mats, general teaching points applicable to the whole class are made. Then those numbered two do the exercise while the teacher coaches and encourages them as individuals. Common teaching points are then made. The pattern is repeated without loss of continuity. After each boy has practised he will be recuperating and by the time his next turn comes along he will be fresh.

d. Coaching The teacher uses his eyes and his voice. He uses his eyes to spot faults and his voice to convey what he requires of the boys. It is important to be positive by telling the boys to do a few key features rather than bewildering them with a list of things not to be done. Positive reinforcement by way of praise for an activity well done or encouragement for doing one's best helps learning and motivates future effort.

The teacher should avoid turning his back to the class. Also, with a class of thirty boys or more, some boys are likely to be slow learners. The teacher has to be patient with the less able, but he can be effective with them if they know what he is looking for. With less complex exercises where the sequence of movement is not too difficult, attention should be given to balance, starting and finishing positions.

The teacher must observe weight-training movements analytically. His verbal instructions must not mislead. For example, he should not suggest that more strength should be exerted in a movement if more speed is required. With a well-cultivated 'teaching eye', the teacher can detect faults early on and put them right before they become ingrained. Correct teaching of beginners is of fundamental importance and cannot be overstressed.

Whole-part-whole Method

With more complicated exercises the 'whole-part-whole' method may have to be used. When teaching with this method a difficult part of the movement is isolated from the whole. It is practised until reasonable, and then incorporated back into the whole movement. The use of this method depends on the individuals in the class.

Phase Method

In addition to the 'whole' or 'whole-part-whole' methods, the 'part' or phase method of teaching may be used. Here the exercise is broken down into parts or phases and learned separately. They are then put together to form a complete movement.

Trial and Error Method

There is a little scope for some trial and error learning of technique, but only in respect of slight adjustments of foot and hand positions or back angles. On no account should safety rules, flat-back techniques, or approved breathing procedures be violated.

Advanced Coaching

Teaching beginners is largely concerned with basic learning. Coaching refines this learning and is applicable to individuals and small groups. Such coaching occurs in the group activities section of a physical education lesson or in a club session.

Equipment appropriate to the activity of the group is used. For example, if the fast lifts are to be practised, then a revolving bar is necessary. With group work, less equipment is required than for class work, but it becomes more specialized.

The various teaching methods already mentioned are used, but the explanation/demonstration/activity/coaching approach is used less often. Groups are arranged according to ability, strength and particular interest.

The introduction of assistance exercises of various kinds becomes necessary with advanced coaching. Not only has the teacher to observe, analyse and coach his pupil's performance mechanically, but he has to consider the part played by other specific factors such as fear, motivation, learning problems and performance plateaux. Matters such as changes in the base of support, joint action, correct sequencing of movement and summation of forces have to be taken into account along with psychological and other factors.

The coach has to give the right verbal cues at the right time to his lifters. He must remember that praise for correct responses is important.

Technically perfect movements in the gymnasium are not enough since they have to be reproduced in competition with its distractions and pressures. If major faults appear when under stress, the coach has to take his pupil right back to the beginning with lighter weights and re-educate the lifter by basic teaching. During training sessions and competitions mutual understanding and respect between the coach and the lifter has to develop if both are to benefit.

Weightlifting Competitions in Schools, Colleges and Clubs

Weightlifting competitions in schools, colleges or clubs are usually based on the Snatch and the Clean and Jerk lifts. For friendly matches other agreed lifts may be used. The rules for the Snatch and Jerk are found in the chapters on those lifts. The rules for other lifts are found in the official weightlifting handbook; in Britain, the rules in the *B.A.W.L.A. Handbook* apply.

It should be noted that the technical rules of the I.P.F. do not permit competition in open or team powerlifting for competitors under sixteen years of age. In any event, powerlifting to maximum for schoolboys (up to sixteen years) is disapproved of.

Competition Procedure

An international pattern barbell, complete with weights and collars, is set out on the centre of the lifting area or platform. Near by is another barbell in the warm-up area. The international bodyweight categories are used for large competitions. The weigh-in should be conducted with scales carrying a current certificate of accuracy. Each lifter is permitted to make three attempts on the Snatch and three attempts on the Jerk. The heaviest successful attempt on the Snatch is added to the heaviest successful attempt on the Jerk to give the lifter's total. The lifter with the highest total is the winner. In the event of a tie, the lightest lifter is declared the winner.

Handicap

For small competitions handicaps may be given. The idea is to give a poundage allowance according to bodyweight. One method is to give the lighter lifter 1 kg (2·2 lb) to be added to his total for every 0·5 kg (1·1 lb) he is lighter than his opponent. (In the imperial system this can be an allowance of 2 lb to be added to a lifter's total for every 1 lb he is lighter than his opponent.) The B.A.W.L.A. also uses the O'Carroll formula for calculating a poundage allowance for a lighter lifter or team.

Attempts

During the competition each lifter specifies the weight at which he proposes to make his first trial. If successful, he must attempt at least

5 kg (11 lb) more (10 lb in the imperial system) for his second attempt. If this is successful, his third and last attempt must be at least 2·5 kg (5½ lb) heavier (5 lb in the imperial system) than his second attempt. A premature increase of 2·5 kg (5½ lb) denotes the last attempt. In no case may a lifter carry out an attempt with a weight less than that employed in the preceding trial. The rest allowed between lifts is normally two minutes. However, if the lifter is taking consecutive lifts, the time allowed between lifts is three minutes.

The rules for the individual lifts are found in the chapters dealing with specific lifts. Additional rules governing championships may be found in the *I.W.F. Handbook* or the *National Weightlifting Association's Handbook.*

It is good training for the non-competitors to act as officials. The teacher can act as the referee. Duties to be performed by others are: M.C., recorder, scoreboard marshall, poundage marshalls, loaders, clerk of scales and timekeeper. Much can be learned by students when they are actively involved in the organization of a weightlifting competition.

Coaching Aids

There are many coaching aids which facilitate the learning of weight-training, weightlifting and related exercises. Also, they are used in the training of coaches. Some coaching aids are listed below.

1. *Blackboard and chalk* are used for diagrams and explanations to illustrate coaching points.
2. *Wallcharts and posters* are useful for display in the weightlifting room or club. They may depict basic weight-training movements, assistance exercises, weightlifting sequences and other movements. The better examples catch the eye to make a quick visual impact and have brief captions carefully worded to make the outline stick. Some charts display data only.
3. *Films, filmloops and slides.* Films of actual championships are valuable coaching material for viewing the techniques of top lifters in action. Also they provide interest and stimulation. Film-loops are usually used for instructional purposes and can be used when analysing weightlifting sequences. Slides are sometimes used to illustrate key positions and data.
4. *Mirrors* are sometimes used by lifters so that they can see their reflections when practising. The side view cannot be seen by the lifter. However, a trained eye is essential if the lifter is to benefit.
5. *Videotape-recorders* are useful for two reasons:
   a. instant feedback of movement is possible, thereby giving knowledge of results which can be used for correction of faults without delay;

   b. standard material for instructional purposes can be replayed over and over again.

6. *Diagnostic aids* are devices used for detecting faults and also for curing them. Large perspex screens with grids and angles are sometimes used to check a lifter's body levers when lifting. A very useful device is the Murray Cross which was developed by Al Murray, B.A.W.L.A. Technical Adviser and former National Coach. This coaching aid is shown in Figure 12. With this aid, a coach can see where a lifter's feet land as well as the relationship of other parts of the body and the bar to his base. Thus the Murray Cross is a particularly useful coaching aid for detecting and rectifying bad balance.

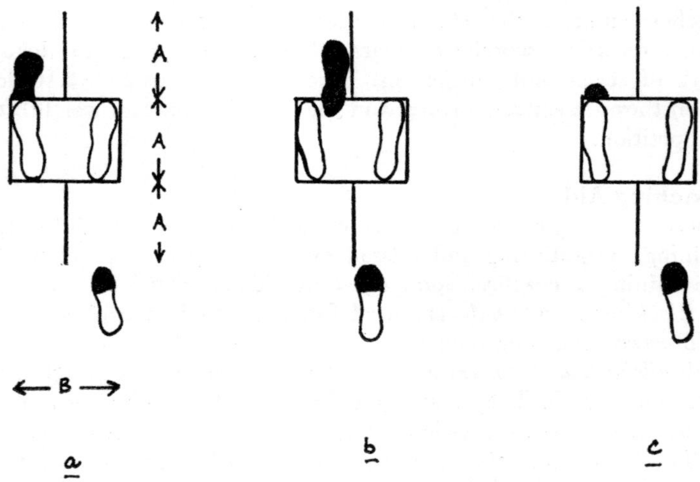

FIGURE 12. The Murray Cross
(A represents the length of the lifter's foot; B is the lifter's hip width. Diagram *a* shows correct foot displacement in the Snatch, whereas *b* and *c* are faulty. In *b* the feet are too close to the centre line. In *c* the front foot is still in the box)

The Russian 'floor grid' is another useful device for observing foot positions and making corrections. It consists of two sets of parallel lines a few centimetres apart at right angles to each other. They are chalked or painted in different colours on the floor or platform. The coach can observe foot deviations and make accurate corrections in a forward-backward direction or sideways.

The Bulgarian electrodinamograph is a recent invention for the automatic recording of the pathway and velocity of the bar. Mathematical and statistical methods enable other parameters such as impulse, power, acceleration and the oscillation of the bar to be calculated. The machine is shown in Plate 3. It has been used to show the two-tempo pulling rhythm of a number of top Bulgarian lifters, the height of pull, the gradient of pull and speed under the bar. Knowledge of such information can be used by the coach—for example, if he knows that the velocity of the barbell in its second phase of the pull is low, then it will be difficult for the lifter to drop quickly under the barbell to the receiving position. The coach can then work with the lifter on the conclusion of the pull and then use the machine to see whether any positive effect has been made on the pull and consequent lowering under the bar.

Fourteen Weightlifting for the Disabled

General Background

Since the Hippocratic era, physical activities have been advocated to augment the treatment of injuries. In 1705, Francis Fuller wrote a book entitled *Medicina gymnastica*, which described how physical exercise could restore power in certain categories of injury. Remedial aspects of the physical education programme were influenced by Ling (1776–1820). More recently, in 1951, Thomas De Lorme and Arthur Watkins wrote an important book, *Progressive resistance exercise*, which described exercises and techniques based upon exercise therapy developed during rehabilitation programmes for wounded soldiers. Heavy weight-training was employed, using ideas and practices arising out of the experiences of weightlifters.

About thirty years ago, sport was not considered appropriate for paralysed persons with disease or injury of the spinal cord. Nowadays, however, remedial exercises and sports such as selected weightlifting developed neuromuscular pathways in the normal parts of the physique, sometimes helping to compensate for functional loss in the paralysed parts. By training with overload principles so that muscles are exercised to the point of fatigue, both muscle size and strength increase. Also, suitable exercise can sometimes help to restore loss of balance. In addition sports exercise produces psychological benefits as well as counteracting mental and physical forms of fatigue. Weightlifting can do this progressively.

Objectives

Recreative or competitive weightlifting of a suitable nature has potential for the physical and psychological rehabilitation of persons suffering from certain disabilities. Weightlifting, in certain cases, can be beneficial in the reintegration of the disabled into society. Thus an important objective of weightlifting for the disabled is to provide and develop recreative and competitive forms of lifting with a view to their competing with each other and sometimes with the able-bodied. Also, social interaction between the able-bodied and disabled is an important objective.

Suitable equipment and facilities must be provided. The disabled require parking facilities near the gymnasium entrance, which should be on the ground floor. Toilets should be roomy and easily accessible.

The use of a competition barbell, special bench and rack are essential. The disabled can achieve a certain degree of activity given the facilities and opportunities.

John Mattick is a quadraplegic (C7) lifter who sustained a cord injury in 1965. Through hard work he has raised his Bench Press to 100 kg (220 lb) at middleweight. He competed in the 1970 Commonwealth Games. He is a shining example for others to copy.

Competitive Weightlifting

The British Sports Association for the Disabled (B.S.A.D.) was established in 1961 by Sir Ludwig Guttman to encourage the disabled to take part in sport as well as to educate others about the importance of sport for the disabled. The B.S.A.D. recognizes weightlifting as a sport for paralysed people in wheelchairs, whether they have an injury or disease of the spinal cord, including poliomyelitis.

The International Stoke Mandeville Games Committee (I.S.M.G.C.) recognizes only the Paraplegic Press on Bench for purposes of international and national competition. This Committee registers World and Continental records on this lift, which differs from the Bench Press for the able-bodied. Important events for the disabled are the Paraplegic Olympic Games, the Paraplegic Commonwealth Games and the Stoke Mandeville Games.

World and Continental records are recognized also on two other lifts which are performed in the supine position. These are the Pull Over and Press on Back and the Lateral Raise, Lying.

For the setting up of a World record an official of the I.S.M.G.C. and an official of the national association of the country to which the lifter belongs must witness the lift. Three registered weightlifting referees must be in attendance to control record attempts. Two or three favourable decisions are necessary in order to pass the lift as valid.

Electrocardiographs must be produced by all lifters taking part in international competitions.

Categories

There are six bodyweight categories for paraplegic weightlifters.

Lightfeatherweight:	up to 51 kg (112¼ lb)
Featherweight:	up to 57 kg (125½ lb)
Lightweight:	up to 65 kg (143¼ lb)
Middleweight:	up to 75 kg (165¼ lb)
Lightheavyweight:	up to 85 kg (187¼ lb)
Heavyweight:	over 85 kg (187¼ lb)

Rules for the Lifts and Methods of Performance

Paraplegic Press on Bench

Official Rules The I.S.M.G.C. rules for the Paraplegic Press on Bench are similar to the I.P.F. rules with the exception of the following.

a. The lifter lies flat on the bench with head, shoulders, buttocks and legs in contact with the bench throughout the lift.
b. The lift starts with the bar 25·5 mm (1 in) from the lifter's chest (as gauged by a measuring stick), and is pressed to arm's length and lowered back to the chest.
c. The lift is not complete until the barbell has been lowered under control to the stands.
d. A lifter subject to severe spasms of his legs may have them fastened to the bench by means of a strap passing over the knees.

The Appendix gives the dimensions of the stands, bench and measuring stick.

Method of Performance The method of performance of this lift is similar to the standard version of the Bench Press where the lifter elects to have his legs on the bench. Often the back cannot be arched as high as the version with the feet on the floor. The disabled lifter has to press the back of his heels into the top of the bench since he cannot press his feet into the floor. Also, he has to practise a controlled lowering to the stands.

Some paraplegic bench pressers inhale on the effort, just as the bar is about to be pressed upward. They exhale on the lowering to the stands.

The lifter's upper arms are not allowed to come into contact with the bench. Any obvious attempt to lift when the barbell is moved along or off the stands is regarded as a failed lift.

Pull Over and Press on Back

Official Rules The lifter lies on his back on the floor, with the centre of the barbell immediately behind his head. The barbell is then brought over his face until the upper arms rest on the floor. The barbell is then pressed to arms' length overhead above the lifter's face.

In the pull over part of the lift, after the barbell has cleared the sternoclavicular joint, the disc weights must not be brought into contact with the floor.

The actual press must be even and continuous. Throughout the lift the shoulders, legs and buttocks shall remain on the floor. There is no restriction on the width between the legs but once the position of the legs has been assumed, they must be kept immobile throughout the lift.

The rules permit the lifter's legs to be held but only for the purpose of maintaining the leg position decided upon before the start of the lift. According to the official rules, padding is forbidden under the lifter's arms or under the barbell.

The referee will signal the start of the lift as soon as he judges that the lifter is in the correct starting position. When the lifter has pressed the barbell to the stipulated finishing position, the referee will signal that the lift is judged as completed.

Method of Performance

a. The lifter lies on his back with his feet placed comfortably apart and held by an assistant if they are likely to move because of muscle spasm or other problems related to his condition. The barbell is on the floor directly behind the lifter's head. It is grasped with the hands equidistant from the centre and spaced about shoulder width apart. The distance between the hands is found by trial and error.
b. The barbell is then rolled towards the head, which is turned sideways. Using this momentum the elbows are bent as the barbell passes the face. The elbows then rest on the floor, while a firm grip is maintained to prevent the barbell from moving backward. The upper arms are usually a little distance away from the sides of the chest.
c. The barbell is pressed upward and slightly backward as fast as possible while the elbows are rotated outward. The locked arms should finish vertically above the shoulder joints. The gravity line of the bar lies over the lifter's chin or the top of his neck.
d. Avoid moving the legs, or lifting the buttocks or shoulders, or allowing the discs to touch the floor during the latter part of the pull over movement.
e. Inhale as the bar is pulled; exhale as the elbows contact the floor on the completion of the pull over. Inhale again as the barbell is pressed; exhale as it is lowered.

LATERAL RAISE, LYING

Official Rules

a. The lifter lies on his back on the floor with the back of his arms on the floor and extended in line with the shoulders. The dumb-bells, which are grasped palms facing upward, are raised in this position until they are directly over the lifter's face.
b. During the lift, the buttocks and legs must remain on the floor, while the arms and legs must be kept straight. There is no restriction on the foot spacing, but once the position of the legs has been assumed, the legs must be kept immobile throughout the lift.
c. The referee will signal the start of the lift as soon as he judges that

the lifter is in the correct starting position. When the lifter has raised the dumb-bells sideways to the stipulated finishing position, the referee will signal that the lift is judged as completed.

d. It should be noted that the official definition permits only the use of dumb-bells—a choice of weights, such as ring weights is not approved. Restrictions on the size of the dumb-bells and disc weights are given in the Appendix.

Method of Performance

a. The lifter lies flat on his back with his feet placed comfortably apart. With arms extended sideways in a straight line with the shoulders, the dumb-bells are grasped with palms uppermost. The handles of the bells may be placed diagonally across the palms, thereby permitting a slightly stronger grip to be taken.
b. Keep the legs straight and ensure there is no movement of the feet. With head, shoulders, feet and buttocks pressing into the floor, raise the dumb-bells in a steady continuous movement until the arms are vertical over the shoulder-joints. Keep the elbows straight throughout the raise.
c. Inhale as the dumb-bells are raised; exhale on lowering them.

Training Methods for Disabled Lifters

Training for paraplegic lifters is not as straightforward as for the able-bodied because of medical complications. Paraplegics tend to have poor cardiovascular efficiency which results in low work tolerance. They tend to lack mobility and have low over-all physical fitness. So great care is essential in training at all stages.

Each lifter may have an individual medical condition, often involving the kidneys, bladder and sometimes the unpleasantness of pressure sores. Training has to fit in with any current treatment.

Beginners

Any paraplegic wishing to start weight-training or lifting movements must seek the approval of his doctor and other medical staff. Any special points to be taken into account such as fatigue, specific weakness and help required should be carefully programmed into the general approach when introducing movements with weights to the disabled person. Sympathetic handling is required, but not to the extent of creating too much dependence of the disabled lifter on his coach. The lifter must be encouraged to do as much as possible for himself. However, he may need a little preliminary assistance in getting on to a bench. Also, the weight will have to be handed to him. If a group of three or more disabled persons can be organized, this is ideal since a businesslike atmosphere can be developed, as well as adequate rest pauses.

The following schedule, using very light weights and concentrating on good style, should be performed during the first four weeks of training.

Warm-up: free exercises in the wheelchair; arm raising upward and backward, with rebound 1 ×10–15; horizontal arm pressing backward, starting out in front, then moved back as far as possible 1 ×10–15; from low arms crossed position, lifting the arms upward and backward 1 ×8–12
Bench Press: 2 ×10—⅓ bodyweight; 3 ×6—⅓ bodyweight plus 5 kg
Press on Back with dumb-bells: 3 ×8—light dumb-bells

Train on the above schedule three times a week, gradually increasing the weights used every two or three weeks. Train on alternate days—for example, Mondays, Wednesdays and Fridays. This enables the lifter to recuperate on non-training days.

Progression

The coach has to judge the lifter's progress and decide when it is in order for the lifter to progress to an intermediate form of training. Usually the beginner's stage goes well although it may take up to six months to handle reasonable weights. If the doctor is satisfied that his patient can safely undertake heavier training loads and the lifter is motivated to do so by his progress, feeling of well-being or interest in competition, then a progression to a training schedule on the following lines is indicated.

Warm-up: free exercises in the wheelchair and on the floor
Bench Press: 2 ×8; 4 ×5
Press on Back with dumb-bells: 4 ×6
Lateral Raise, Lying (light dumb-bells): 3 ×8 (intensity determined by trial and error)

Train three times weekly on alternate days. Gradually increase the weight of the bells every two or three weeks. Try for a maximum poundage every four to six weeks. Follow this by a week's 'active rest' using 50 per cent of maximum.

The Press on Back with dumb-bells can be substituted by the Pull Over and Press on Back with barbell. This is a different movement which will provide variety. The use of incentives such as participating in the Certificate of Merit Scheme is recommended.

Advanced Training

After several months of intermediate training, the paraplegic lifter may wish to enter one of the various competitions open to him. He usually starts by competing at the sports day of his own hospital.

Preparation for this consists of stepping up the intermediate training—lower repetitions with heavier weights are used, but these should not be overdone. Work up to two or three single lifts once a week.

Uninterrupted long-term planning is virtually impossible because of medical problems and their treatment, so a series of miniature schedules is usually prescribed. These will vary according to the individual. 'Peaking up' is a problem because of treatment.

The following schedule was used by lightheavyweight, Ralph Rowe, prior to his winning the gold medal in his class at the 1974 Commonwealth Games in Christchurch, New Zealand. The aim was to be in peak form at the Games. So a simple training microcycle of nine weeks' duration was prepared. Working back in three phases of three weeks each, progressive increases in weight in each phase were prescribed. Training occurred three times weekly with rest days in between. There were two heavy sessions per week, interspersed with a light session for recovery purposes.

Weeks 9–7 before the Championships

Monday

Bench Press: 2 × 8—60 kg (132¼ lb), warm-up; 2 × 8—90 kg (198¼ lb); 2 × 6—110 kg (242½ lb); 3 × 4—120 kg (264½ lb); 3 × 3—132·5 kg (292 lb); 2 × 3—147·5 kg (325 lb); 3 × 1—157·5 kg (347 lb)

Wednesday

Bench Press: 2 × 8—60 kg (132¼ lb), warm-up; 2 × 8—90 kg (198¼ lb); 2 × 6—110 kg (242½ lb)

Press on Back with dumb-bells: 6 × 8—2 × 45 kg (99 lb)

Friday as for Monday

Weeks 6–4 before the Championships

Monday

Bench Press: 2 × 8—60 kg (132¼ lb), warm-up; 2 × 8—90 kg (198¼ lb); 2 × 4—110 kg (242½ lb); 2 × 3—150 kg (330½ lb); 2 × 2—160 kg (352½ lb); 3 × 1—172·5 kg (380¼ lb)

Wednesday

Bench Press: 2 × 8—60 kg (132¼ lb), warm-up; 2 × 8—90 kg (198¼ lb); 2 × 6—110 kg (242½ lb)

Press on Back with dumb-bells: 6 × 6—2 × 55 kg (121¼ lb)

Friday as for Monday

Weeks 3–1 before the Championships

Monday

Bench Press: 2 × 8—60 kg (132¼ lb), warm-up; 2 × 8—90 kg

(198¼ lb); 2 × 4—115 kg (253½ lb); 2 × 4—137·5 kg (303 lb); 2 × 3—152·5 kg (336 lb); 2 × 2—165 kg (363¾ lb); 2 × 2—175 kg (385¾ lb); 3 × 1—180 kg (396¾ lb)

Wednesday

Bench Press: 2 × 8—60 kg (132¼ lb), warm-up; 2 × 8—90 kg (198¼ lb); 2 × 6—110 kg (242½ lb)

Press on Back with dumb-bells: 6 × 3—2 × 60 kg (132¼ lb)

Friday as for Monday

There are many sports organizations the disabled can join or seek further information. The following indicates some of these associations:

The British Paraplegic Sports Society Ltd., Stoke Mandeville Sports Stadium for the Paralysed and other Disabled, Harvey Road, Aylesbury, Buckinghamshire. *Telephone:* Aylesbury 84848

The British Sports Association for the Disabled, Stoke Mandeville Sports Stadium for the Paralysed and other Disabled, Harvey Road, Aylesbury, Buckinghamshire. *Telephone:* Aylesbury 84848

U.S.A.

National Paraplegia Foundation, 333N Michigan Avenue, Chicago, Illinois 60601. *Telephone:* (312) 346–4779

Canada

Canadian Paraplegia Association, 520 Sutherland Drive, Toronto, Ontario M4G 3V9

Appendix

Dimensions of Apparatus for Paraplegic Weightlifting

Bench The bench will be made of wood. It should be strong, and meet the following requirements.

Width 61 cm (24 in); height 46 cm (18 in); width where head and shoulders lie 30·5 cm (12 in). This part of the bench shall be 76 cm (30 in) long—over-all length being 213·5 cm (84 in).

Stands The stands shall be made of tubular and angled steel, and of a similar design to the ones used at Stoke Mandeville Games.

The stands must be telescopic, have a minimum height of 61 cm (24 in) and adjust to fixed positions at 6·35 mm ($\frac{1}{4}$ in) intervals. Each stand should be built on to a solid piece of wood 5 cm (2 in) thick. The stands shall conform to the following requirements.

Bases should be 91·5 cm (36 in) long, 38 cm (15 in) wide and 5 cm (2 in) thick. Tubular uprights should have 56 cm (22 in) centre when mounted on the base. The top supporting bar should be rubber-covered and should be 76 cm (30 in) long and 5 cm (2 in) wide and made of angled steel for rigidity.

Measuring Stick The measuring stick shall be a plain piece of wood measuring 25·5 mm (1 in) by 25·5 mm (1 in) by 305·5 mm (12 in).

Dumb-bells Dumb-bells shall not exceed 61 cm (24 in) in length. The distance between the disc weights shall be not more than 30·5 cm (12 in). The maximum size of the disc weights shall be 28 cm (11 in).

Further Reading

The following publications are recommended for those who wish to further their knowledge on different topics related to weightlifting:

Anatomy

Rasch, P. J. and Burke R. K. (1963) *Kinesiology and Applied Anatomy*. Henry Kimpton, London.

British Amateur Weightlifters' Association

Contact the General Secretary: W. W. R. Holland, O.B.E., F.A.D.O., 3 Iffley Turn, Oxford, OX4 4DY.

Circuit Training and Physical Fitness

Morgan, R. E. and Adamson, G. T. (1957) *Circuit Training*. G. Bell and Sons Ltd., London.

Cureton, T. K. (1941) 'Flexibility as an Aspect of Physical Fitness'. Supplement to *Research Quarterly*, 12, 381–90.

General

Webster, D. P. (1976) *The Iron Game—An Illustrated History of Weightlifting*. Geddes, Irvine, Scotland.

Williams, J. G. P. (1965) *Medical Aspects of Sport and Physical Fitness*. Pergamon Press, London.

Measurement

Fleischman, E. A. (1964) *The Structure and Measurement of Physical Fitness*. Prentice-Hall, Inc., Englewood Cliffs, New Jersey.

Clarke, H. H. (1959) *Application of Measurement to Health and Physical Education*. Prentice-Hall.

Mechanics

Dyson, G. H. G. (1962) *The Mechanics of Athletics*. University of London Press.

Physiology

McNaught, A. B. and Collander, R. (1965) *Illustrated Physiology*. E. and S. Livingstone Ltd., Edinburgh and London.

Powerlifting

Lear, P. J. and Leggett, G. (1977) *Manual of Powerlifting*. Tripod Press Ltd., Leamington Spa.

Skill

Knapp, E. (1963) *Skill in Sport*. Routledge and Kegan Paul, London.

Strength

De Lorme, T. S. and Watkins, A. L. (1951) *Progressive Resistance Exercise*. Appleton-Century-Crofts, Inc., New York.

Strength & Motor Learning

Brown, C. R. and Kenyon, G. S. (editors) (1968) *Classical Studies on Physical Activity*. Prentice-Hall, Inc., Englewood Cliffs, New Jersey.

Ikai, M. and Steinhams, S. (1961) *Some Factors Modifying the Expression of Human Strength*. J. Appl. Physiol. 16, 157.

Weight-Training

Murray, A. (1971) *Modern Weight-Training*. Kaye and Ward, London.

Weightlifting

B.A.W.L.A. (1975) *Know the game: Weightlifting*. E.P. Publishing Ltd., Wakefield.

B.A.W.L.A. *Handbook for Instructors*.

Lukyanov, M. T. and Falameev, A. E. (1973) Vdigane na Tezhesti za Yunoshi, Sofia.

O'Carroll, M. J. (1968) *On the Relation Between Strength and Bodyweight*. Research in Physical Education, Vol 1, No. 3.

Strength Athlete. Official B.A.W.L.A. Journal. Ed. Kirkley, G. Modern Sport Pub. Co., 197 Clive Road, W. Dulwich, London, SE 21 8DG.

Vorobyev, A. H. (1977) Tyazheloatletichesky Sport: Ocherki po Fisiologii i Sportivnoy Trenirovke. Moscow.

Webster, D. P. and Murray, A. (1964) *Defying Gravity*. Modern Sport Pub. Co., London.

Webster, D. P. and Murray, A. (1967) *The Two Hands' Snatch*. Modern Sport Pub. Co., London.

Webster, D. P. (1967) *Lifting Illustrated*. Modern Sport Pub. Co., London.

Index

Adamson, G., 24
Alexeev, 22, 29
Anderson, P., 94

Basanowski, 94
Bottino, 16
British Amateur Weightlifting Association, 15, 17, 19, 124
British Medical Profession and safety, 38
British Sports Association for the Disabled, 129
Bulgarian weightlifting, 17, 127

Clark, H. Harrison, 24
Creus, J., 16
Cuban weightlifting, 17
Cureton, 26

De Lorme and Watkins, 28, 128

East Germany, 37, 38

Falameev, A., 78, 89
Finland, 38
Fleishman, 24
Fuller, Francis, 128

George, Pete, 37
Guttman, Sir Ludwig, 129

Halliday, J., 16
Hungarian split workout, 77, 78

International Powerlifting Federation, 15, 94, 95, 99
International Stoke Mandeville Games, 129, 130
International Weightlifting Federation, 15, 40, 47, 62, 90, 91, 125

Japan, 38
Jokl, 28

Karonov, 36
Kailajarvi, 38
Kereszty, 86, 91
Knapp, 35
Kono, T., 23
Kraus, 26

Ling, 128

Martin, Louis, 70
Mattick, J., 129
McKenzie, P., 16, 29, 113
Morgan and Adamson, 24
Munchinger, 38
Murray, Al, 70, 126

Nassiri, 29

O'Carroll Formula, 124

Reidhoudt, 29
Rowe, Ralph, 134

Sedgewick, 25
Smalcerz, 16
Steinhouse and Ikai, 23
Sweden, 37

Terlazzo, 16

Valsalva phenomenon, 39

U.S.S.R., 16, 17
  lifters, 52
  research, 34
  training principle, 78

Walters, 28
Webster, D. P., 50, 53